**Editorial Project Manager**
Erica N. Russikoff, M.A.

**Editor in Chief**
Karen J. Goldfluss, M.S. Ed.

**Creative Director**
Sarah M. Fournier

**Cover Artist**
Sarah Kim

**Illustrator**
Mark Mason

**Art Coordinator**
Renée Mc Elwee

**Imaging**
Amanda R. Harter
Leonard P. Swierski

**Publisher**
Mary D. Smith, M.S. Ed.

* Explores narrative, opinion/argumentative, and informative/explanatory writing
* Introduces diverse writing selections for modeling and analysis
* Targets essential paragraph features and critical essay components
* Encourages feedback through peer reviews, self-evaluations, and teacher input
* Lexile levels and standards correlations provided

OPINION
INFORMATIVE
NARRATIVE

Teacher Created Resources

**Author**
Tracie I. Heskett, M. Ed.

For correlations to the Common Core State Standards, see pages 157–160 of this book or visit *http://www.teachercreated.com/standards/*.

Cover photograph credits:
* Playground, ©Greg Goebel (*https://www.flickr.com/photos/37467370@N08/18909879490/*), CC BY-SA 2.0.
* Mt. Rainier National Park, ©liquidcrash (*https://www.flickr.com/photos/124320023@N06/14703351820/*), CC BY-SA 2.0.
* Solar Panels, ©Marufish (*https://www.flickr.com/photos/marufish/8340312387/*), CC BY-SA 2.0.

**Teacher Created Resources**
12621 Western Avenue
Garden Grove, CA 92841
www.teachercreated.com
ISBN: 978-1-4206-8013-3
© *2017 Teacher Created Resources*
Made in U.S.A.

Teacher Created Resources

# Table of Contents

# Introduction

*The Write Stuff* is a series designed to help students build strong foundational skills in writing. To master the skills needed to write effectively, students benefit from guided instruction, analysis of writing models, and writing for a variety of audiences. The books in this series guide both teachers and students through the process of writing as it relates to three specific writing formats.

This book provides writing samples for students to study, as well as opportunities for students to write their own pieces. Students receive feedback on their writing in a variety of ways. They participate in peer reviews, complete self-evaluations, receive evaluations from the teacher, and compare differences in these assessments of their writing.

## About This Book

**Sections:** The book is divided into three main sections, one for each type of writing students need to learn for college and career readiness: Opinion/Argumentative Writing, Informative/Explanatory Writing, and Narrative Writing.

**THREE SECTIONS**

**Opinion/Argumentative Writing**
- Paragraph Module
- Essay Module

**Informative/Explanatory Writing**
- Paragraph Module
- Essay Module

**Narrative Writing**
- Paragraph Module
- Essay Module

**Themed Modules:** Each section has two modules, or in-depth units.

*First Module:* This module presents a series of step-by-step lessons to introduce students to and teach the characteristics of that type of writing. Students read and discuss strong and weak examples of the type of writing in focus. Reading passages fall within the fourth-grade reading range based on Lexile estimates (740L–940L) for this grade level. Students then model what they learned to write a piece in that specific genre, from opening sentence to conclusion.

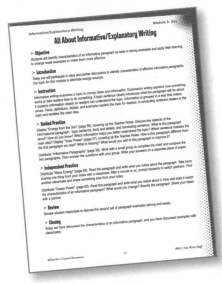

Lesson Plan

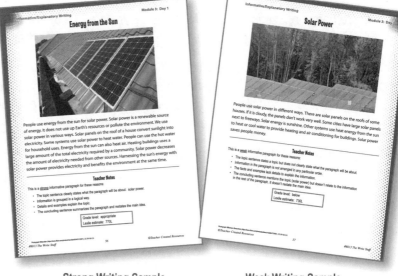

Strong Writing Sample                    Weak Writing Sample

*Second Module:* This module provides additional experiences in which students learn about and practice writing a longer piece, or essay, in the focus genre. Each module suggests a topic for student writing. Additional related writing topics are listed at the back of the book on pages 155–156.

> Note: Modules 1, 3, and 5 require 10 days or class periods to complete, while Modules 2, 4, and 6 require seven days.

A chart on pages 157–160 lists the Common Core State Standards addressed in each lesson.

# How to Use This Book

Each module includes writing samples written below, at, and above grade level as indicated. Lessons suggest how to incorporate the writing samples, although you may use them in other ways for additional practice. For example, conduct a shared-writing activity in which students work together as a class to mimic a sample paragraph about the same or a different topic. Alternatively, have students work with a partner to strengthen an example of a weak paragraph. Students may also work independently to practice writing paragraphs using one or more strong examples as a model.

When instructed, use a document camera or make photocopies onto transparencies (for overhead projectors) to display text. Cover the Teacher Notes with a piece of paper as needed during class discussion.

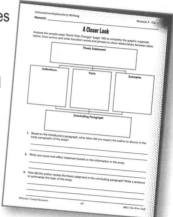

Each lesson begins with a scripted lesson plan. The script for the teacher is presented in italicized font. These lesson plans inform teachers about what to expect students to learn and be able to do. They enable teachers to make the best use of the time they have available for teaching writing in an already busy school day. The lessons include strategies that effectively help students learn to write.

Within each module, student activities build on one another. Answers to activities are provided in the lesson plan. Students focus on a single topic throughout the module as they work toward a finished product. You may wish to have students keep their activity pages in a folder for reference as they complete each lesson. Alternatively, you may refer to the related topics on pages 155–156 to give students additional writing experiences during lesson activities.

Guided Practice provides opportunities for students to work together as a whole class, in small groups, or with partners to focus on a particular aspect of the writing type in focus. Independent Practice offers additional activities for students to apply new skills as they write one or more parts of the work in progress.

Each module has one lesson in which students participate in a peer-review activity. Encourage students to offer positive feedback as well as constructive criticism that will motivate their classmates to improve their writing.

Students complete a self-evaluation activity during each module and then later compare the scores they assigned their own writing with scores they receive on a teacher evaluation. Rubrics provide objective statements about writing that help students analyze and reflect on their work with the goal of creating written selections that are more effective and engaging for readers.

Some activities ask students to research their topics. Refer to the following topic overview chart to plan and provide appropriate research resources.

## ➤ Topics Overview

| | | |
|---|---|---|
| Opinion/Argumentative | Module 1 | Public Parks |
| Opinion/Argumentative | Module 2 | New Transportation Technology |
| Informative/Explanatory | Module 3 | Alternate Energy Sources |
| Informative/Explanatory | Module 4 | Polar Change and Exploration |
| Narrative | Module 5 | Drones |
| Narrative | Module 6 | Weather-Related Experiences |

# All About Opinion/Argumentative Writing

## ➤ Objective

Students will demonstrate an understanding of argumentative writing that states an opinion and supports it with valid reasoning and relevant evidence by identifying strong and weak examples of such writing.

## ➤ Introduction

*Today we will think about the characteristics of effective opinion writing. You will read sample opinion pieces that state a viewpoint about public parks, which is the topic for this module.* (Teacher note: Fourth-graders may visit national parks for free. For more information, visit *https://everykidinapark.gov/.*)

## ➤ Instruction

*A strong opinion piece provides reasons and evidence to support the opinion. The conclusion helps readers understand why the stated opinion is valid and may encourage readers to change their beliefs or take action.*

## ➤ Guided Practice

Distribute "Understanding Opinion Writing" (page 6). Display "People Enjoy Safe Parks" (strong example, page 7), covering up the Teacher Notes. *Look at the sample opinion piece displayed and follow along as I read. Which characteristics of opinion writing do you notice in the writing?* Guide students to identify the stated opinion, reasons and evidence to support the opinion, and the strengths of the concluding sentence. Then let them complete the first portion of Part One of the activity. *Let's read together another example of opinion writing. How is it similar to or different from the first piece we read?* Display "Parks Make Healthy Communities" (weak example, page 8), covering up the Teacher Notes, and discuss. *Now complete the remainder of Part One of the activity.*

## ➤ Independent Practice

*Now you will read two more samples of opinion writing, decide which piece is more effective, and complete the graphic organizer in Part Two of the activity.* Distribute the second set of writing samples on pages 9–10.

## ➤ Review

*What are the three characteristics we identified in a strong opinion piece? Are there any other characteristics you noticed?*

## ➤ Closing

*Today we discussed characteristics of opinion writing. You read samples of opinion pieces that demonstrate what makes this type of writing effective.*

## ➤ Answers

"Understanding Opinion Writing" (page 6): Part One—This type of writing <u>states an opinion</u> (or <u>states the author's viewpoint</u>) about a topic. It gives <u>reasons</u> and <u>evidence</u> to <u>support</u> the topic sentence. The concluding sentence may ask <u>readers</u> to <u>change</u> their beliefs or take <u>action</u>. Part Two—*topic sentence*: Mt. Rainier National Park is one of my favorite places because it has something for everyone; reasons or evidence: Answers will vary but can be found in sentences 2–8; concluding sentence: Everyone should try to visit this park that people of all ages and abilities can enjoy.

**Name(s):** _____

# Understanding Opinion Writing

➤ **Part One**

Read the opinion piece on page 7. Then complete the sentences below. *Note:* Some lines require more than one word.

This type of writing _____ about a topic.

It gives _____ and _____ to _____ the topic sentence.

The concluding sentence may ask _____ to _____ their

beliefs or take _____.

Now read the opinion piece on page 8. Which opinion piece is more effective? Why?

_____

_____

_____

_____

_____

➤ **Part Two**

Read the opinion pieces on pages 9 and 10. Complete the graphic organizer below with information from the stronger opinion piece.

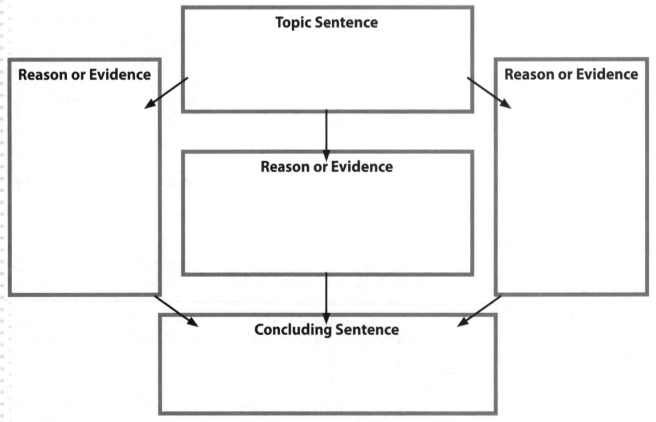

# People Enjoy Safe Parks

Parks provide a place for kids to enjoy themselves, but it is also important for parks to have safety features. If too many people get hurt, kids will not be able to go to the park anymore. For example, skaters in a skate park need to be able to see one another. Playground equipment should have a thick layer of bark chips to protect kids when they fall. Another way to stay safe is to keep parks free of crime. Good lighting and signs show people how to find their way around a park. They feel safe when they know where to find important locations in a park. When a park is safe, more people will use it and enjoy nature.

---

## Teacher Notes

This is a <u>strong</u> paragraph for these reasons:

- The topic sentence clearly states an opinion.
- The author gives reasons with evidence and examples, including details.
- The concluding sentence restates the opinion and summarizes the reasoning.

> Grade level:  appropriate
> Lexile estimate:  910L

# Parks Make Healthy Communities

Our neighborhood needs a well-planned community park. Anyone could come and enjoy the park because it would be free. A park has lots of grass and trails and a playground area. People enjoy exploring hiking trails in state parks. A park is a good way to get exercise without belonging to a gym. Families could spend time together and have fun. If the park was in our neighborhood, it would be close enough to walk so people could go there often. People would be healthier if we had a new park in our neighborhood.

## Teacher Notes

This is a <u>weak</u> paragraph for these reasons:

- The title does not relate to the rest of the paragraph.
- The topic sentence has a vague opinion: "Our neighborhood needs a well-planned community park."
- The reasons relate to the topic but do not explain why the author holds this opinion.
- The reasons are not presented in a logical order.
- The examples do not directly support a reason.
- The concluding sentence does not relate to the stated opinion.
- The concluding sentence does not ask readers to change their thinking or take action.

> Grade level: appropriate
> Lexile estimate: 750L

**Name(s):** _____

# A Favorite Place: Mt. Rainier National Park

Mt. Rainier National Park is one of my favorite places because it has something for everyone. The drive to the visitor area has many awesome views of the mountain. The visitor area has an information center with photos and interesting exhibits. There is a picnic area where people can sit and enjoy the scenery. We wanted to hike and found a trail that wasn't too difficult for our first day out. Along the trail we saw a waterfall and close-up views of the glacier. Visitors can take a scenic drive up to a different visitor center that has a wildflower viewing area. Along the drive there are waterfalls and majestic views of mountains in the distance. The visitor center provides maps for short, easy walks or longer hikes. Everyone should try to visit this park that people of all ages and abilities can enjoy.

---

### Teacher Notes
Grade level:  appropriate
Lexile estimate:  880L

---

**Name(s):** _____

# My Favorite State Park

Last summer, my family went to Niagara Falls. It is a famous park in New York State. I enjoyed our visit because I like waterfalls. The roar of the water cascading over the cliff was so loud we could hardly hear each other talk. We walked down to see a second, smaller waterfall, too. Other features of the park include a rock-climbing wall and a theater. Everyone should visit this park that is also a national heritage area.

### Teacher Notes

Grade level: appropriate
Lexile estimate: 740L

# Topic Sentences

## ➤ Objective

Students will learn characteristics of effective topic sentences, identify such sentences, and practice writing their own topic sentences.

## ➤ Introduction

*Today we will talk about topic sentences, and you will identify topic sentences in sample paragraphs. Then you will select a topic and practice writing a topic sentence.*

## ➤ Instruction

*A topic sentence introduces what the paragraph will be about in an interesting way. The author clearly states his or her opinion about the topic. It is usually the first sentence, but not always. Interesting topic sentences catch the readers' attention and raise questions in their minds, drawing them in so they want to read more.*

## ➤ Guided Practice

*To identify the topic sentence in a paragraph, think about what the paragraph is about. Authors will also state an opinion, or what they think or believe about the topic.* Distribute "Topic Sentences that Stand Out" (page 12) and different-colored highlighters. Work through the first example together as a class. Support students as they complete B and C on their own. *What topics did the author(s) write about in their paragraphs?*

## ➤ Independent Practice

*Now you will have time to practice writing topic sentences.* Distribute "My Opinion About Parks" (page 13). *Think about what you will write about and your opinion of the topic.*

## ➤ Review

Review the characteristics of an effective topic sentence (introduces topic, hooks the reader), using the sample paragraphs as examples. *What is unique about a topic sentence in an opinion piece?* (It states an opinion about the topic.)

## ➤ Closing

*Today we identified topic sentences in sample paragraphs. You practiced writing topic sentences to introduce your opinion about parks.*

## ➤ Answers

"Topic Sentences that Stand Out" (page 12):

> A—*topic:* community parks; *stated opinion:* provide a great legacy
>
> B—*topic:* Yosemite National Park; *stated opinion:* beautiful natural area that I want to visit
>
> C—*topic:* Mt. Rushmore; *stated opinion:* the most unusual [park]

"My Opinion About Parks" (page 13): Check student writing for topic, statement of opinion, and topic sentence.

Name(s): _____

# Topic Sentences that Stand Out

Read each paragraph and decide which sentence is the topic sentence. Highlight the part of the sentence that tells what the paragraph is about in one color. Use a different color to highlight the part of the sentence that states the author's opinion.

**A.** Community parks provide a great legacy for us. A city or county government may establish a local park. Land is set aside for public use and enjoyment. No one can build houses or businesses on the land. Parks preserve scenery and wildlife habitats, which are good for the environment. Visitors can view plants and animals in their natural state. It is healthy and relaxing for people to be outside in nature. Today thousands of people visit state and community parks. They participate in various activities, such as sightseeing and hiking. It's up to us to take care of this legacy. Then the next generation can also enjoy the beauty of our parks.

**B.** Yosemite National Park in California is a beautiful natural area that draws thousands of visitors each year, and one day I want to be one of them. Pictures of the park show beautiful scenery, including majestic rock cliffs and spectacular waterfalls. I imagine having a picnic and taking my own photographs of the sights. Perhaps I would even see wildlife! The activity I look forward to the most at Yosemite, though, is hiking one of the many trails in the park. This park appears to have something for everyone.

**C.** My family has visited several parks, and Mt. Rushmore in South Dakota was one of the most unusual. This popular park has the faces of four presidents carved in stone cliffs. The carvings depict George Washington, Thomas Jefferson, Abraham Lincoln, and Theodore Roosevelt. Visitors can learn about the creation of the sculptures and the tools the workers used. The most interesting part was standing on the mountain and looking out over the plains—40 miles in one direction!

---

### Teacher Notes

A—Grade level: below; Lexile estimate: 730L

B—Grade level: appropriate; Lexile estimate: 820L

C—Grade level: appropriate; Lexile estimate: 890L

---

**Name(s):** _____

# My Opinion About Parks

A topic sentence introduces the topic and states the author's opinion about it. To write a topic sentence, think of what the paragraph will be about. What is your opinion about the topic? Think about what you want to say about it.

## ➤ Part One

Read the list of suggested topics below. Select one that you have a definite opinion about. Then complete the sentences.

- the benefits of community parks
- a favorite park you have visited
- an unusual park you have seen or heard about
- activities you enjoy in a park
- your favorite type of park to visit
- why your community needs more parks
- how our parks could be improved

1. My paragraph will be about _____
   *(topic)*
   _____.

2. I want to say that _____
   *(opinion statement)*
   _____

   _____.

## ➤ Part Two

**topic + opinion statement = topic sentence**

Rewrite the two sentences you wrote in Part One as one interesting topic sentence.

_____

_____

_____

# Supporting Details

## ➤ Objective

Students will group related details that support a topic sentence, think about details to support the opinions of their topic sentences, and receive feedback from peers.

## ➤ Introduction

*It is important to include details to support the opinion that is stated in the topic sentence in opinion writing. You will work with a small group to organize details in a sample paragraph and then think about sensory details to include in your opinion writing.*

## ➤ Instruction

*People might be more likely to change their beliefs or behavior to agree with an author's opinion when it is well supported with reasons that include facts and details. Readers want to know why they should think or act a certain way. Effective argumentative writing supports the opinion in the topic sentence with facts and details that make sense.*

## ➤ Guided Practice

*Which features should be included in parks for kids?* Distribute "So Many Reasons" (page 15) to small groups. *Read the topic sentence and possible reasons that might be included in this opinion paragraph about park features. Work with your small group to determine which ideas go together. Discuss with classmates additional facts and details to support the topic sentence and add these reasons to the list in their appropriate categories.*

## ➤ Independent Practice

*Thinking about the five senses helps authors include details in their writing. Specific facts also contribute to reasons why an author might hold a particular opinion.* Distribute "Using My Senses" (page 16). *Using "My Opinion About Parks" (page 13), complete the chart on page 16 to think about a community park and the features you believe such a park should have.*

## ➤ Review

Review "So Many Reasons" to check for understanding of grouping related ideas. *Which facts and details did your group add to each category? How do these support the topic sentence?*

## ➤ Closing

*Today you have grouped facts and details into related categories, or reasons, to support a topic sentence. You have also brainstormed facts and details to support your opinion about the features of a community park and received feedback from a classmate.*

## ➤ Answers

"So Many Reasons" (page 15): *suggested categories*—play equipment 1, 2, 6, 7, 10; water 3, 4, 5, 8, 9

Name(s): _____

# So Many Reasons

Read the topic sentence of a paragraph about park features. Then read the list of reasons that support the opinion.

Which two main categories would you use to organize the information below?

**Topic Sentence:** Our community needs a park that has play equipment, grassy fields, and water so everyone can enjoy themselves.

**Reasons:**

(1) Play equipment and grass give kids ways to exercise.

(2) Some kids like the play equipment the best.

(3) Water helps people relax and have fun.

(4) Water activities are fun on warm days.

(5) If there is water in a park, there can be boats for people who don't want to swim.

(6) Interesting play equipment makes a park more exciting.

(7) Children can make up games to play on the equipment and in the grassy areas.

(8) Some community parks take advantage of water in natural areas, such as creeks, rivers, or lakes.

(9) Parks in urban areas can include water activities by having an open fountain area.

(10) Kids learn new skills and use problem solving on playground equipment.

Label the boxes below with category names appropriate for the reasons listed above. Then write the number next to each sentence in its correct category.

<br>

_____     _____

_____     _____

# Using My Senses

Use the information from "My Opinion About Parks" (page 13) to complete the activity.

1. Write your topic sentence from the activity.

   _____

   _____

2. Close your eyes and picture the park in your topic sentence.

3. Use the chart below to describe your mental picture of the park. In the first column, list the features in the park that you will write about. In the next column, write the sense(s) this feature engages (e.g., sight, sound, touch, smell). Then describe specific details about the feature in the third column. Add additional facts about the feature as needed in the fourth column. Use the final column to summarize the reason this feature is included in the park.

| Feature | Sense | Details | Facts | Reason |
|---------|-------|---------|-------|--------|
|         |       |         |       |        |
|         |       |         |       |        |
|         |       |         |       |        |
|         |       |         |       |        |
|         |       |         |       |        |

4. Exchange papers with a classmate. Read the facts and details listed for your classmate's topic sentence. Draw a picture on the back of this page to show how you envision the park your classmate describes, including as many details as possible. Discuss with your partner to compare your perceptions with his or her opinions and reasons.

5. After you hear your partner's feedback, read over your facts and details. What could you add to make your reasons more strongly support the opinion in your topic sentence?

   _____

   _____

   _____

# Linking Words

## ➤ Objective

Students will practice creating sentences that incorporate linking words and phrases to connect reasons to the opinions in their topic sentences.

## ➤ Introduction

*Today we will practice using words and phrases to connect the opinion in a topic sentence with an author's reasons for having that opinion.*

## ➤ Instruction

*Effective opinion writing includes reasons that support an opinion. Reasons explain why the author feels or thinks a certain way about a topic. Convincing reasons often include specific facts or details. Writers use linking words or phrases to connect reasons, facts, and details to the opinion in the topic sentence, so it all makes sense.*

## ➤ Guided Practice

*Listen as I read aloud words and phrases that we use to connect reasons to an opinion.* Read aloud:  *for instance, in order to, in addition. What other words have you learned that can link reasons and opinions?* Discuss (suggested): *because, since, for example. Let's think together of a topic sentence about parks.* Discuss and write a topic sentence together as a class. *What are some reasons someone might hold this opinion?* List student-generated reasons on a whiteboard or chart paper.

*Let's read each reason as a sentence using an appropriate word or phrase to connect it to our topic sentence.* As class volunteers read aloud, students will write linking words/phrases to create a complete sentence.

## ➤ Independent Practice

Distribute "Reasons for My Opinion" (page 18). *On your activity page, you will see linking words and phrases. Write your topic sentence from "My Opinion About Parks" (page 13), and then list your reasons. Practice writing sentences using words and phrases to connect your reasons to your opinion.*

## ➤ Review

*Read your sentences to a partner. Discuss examples in which you used linking words correctly and consider changes you could make to strengthen your sentences and paragraph to make it easier for readers to understand.*

## ➤ Closing

*Today we practiced using words and phrases to connect a topic sentence with related reasons.*

Name(s): _____

# Reasons for My Opinion

Use the information from "My Opinion About Parks" (page 13) to complete the activity.

1. Write your topic sentence about parks from the activity.

   _____

   _____

2. List reasons, facts, and details to support why you have this opinion about parks.

   _____

   _____

   _____

   _____

   _____

   _____

   _____

3. The following words and phrases may be used to connect a topic sentence with related reasons, including facts and details.

   | | | |
   |---|---|---|
   | because | for instance | in order to |
   | for example | in addition | since |

   Use the words and phrases in the box above to write sentences using the reasons you listed in #2.

   _____

   _____

   _____

   _____

   _____

   _____

   _____

4. Number your sentences to show the order in which you would write them in a paragraph. If time allows, write the sentences in order as an opinion paragraph on a separate piece of paper.

# Concluding Sentences

## ➤ Objective

Students will read sample concluding sentences, discuss what makes them effective, and write concluding sentences for their own and a partner's writing.

## ➤ Introduction

*We have learned about characteristics of effective opinion writing. Now it's time to think about how to conclude, or finish, the opinion paragraph.*

## ➤ Instruction

*A strong concluding sentence restates the topic and opinion that were expressed in the topic sentence. One way to do this is to focus on the main idea. A concluding sentence may state why the author holds the stated opinion or why he or she wrote the piece.*

## ➤ Guided Practice

Distribute "Opinions and Concluding Sentences" (page 20). *In your small group, work together to write a concluding sentence that restates the main idea and why the author wrote the piece for each topic sentence in Part One. As a group, discuss which of your concluding sentences is the strongest or most convincing and why. Work together to evaluate the concluding sentences in Part Two. Use your ideas about what makes a strong concluding sentence to revise one or more of the concluding sentences your group wrote in Part One.*

## ➤ Independent Practice

*There are different ways to approach writing a concluding sentence. Let's look at some of those ways.* Distribute "Restating or Explaining" (page 21) and review 1–3 together with students. *For each number, you will write a different concluding sentence. For each statement you write, think about the opinion you stated in your topic sentence on "My Opinion About Parks" (page 13). Read your completed statements and draw a star by the concluding sentence you think is the most effective. Then answer #4. Complete Part Two with a partner.*

## ➤ Review

*What have you learned about writing a concluding sentence? How would you describe an effective concluding sentence?*

## ➤ Closing

*You have practiced reading and writing concluding sentences, and have thought about possible concluding sentences for your own opinion piece.*

## ➤ Answers

"Opinions and Concluding Sentences" (page 20): *Part Two*—Reasons may include restating the opinion, summarizing the main idea, explaining the purpose or reason why the author wrote the piece, a call to action, or encouragement for readers to change their thinking or behavior.

Name(s): _____

# Opinions and Concluding Sentences

## ➤ Part One

Write a concluding sentence for each topic sentence. Restate the main idea and summarize why the author has this opinion.

**1.** Amusement parks provide excellent entertainment for families.

_____

_____

**2.** National historic sites offer visitors valuable and interesting information about the past.

_____

_____

**3.** I am fortunate to have parents who love to travel and take our family to many national parks.

_____

_____

**4.** The arboretum has beautiful walking paths that appeal to people of all ages and abilities.

_____

_____

## ➤ Part Two

Below are several concluding sentences. Write one reason why each statement is an effective concluding sentence.

**1.** Not everyone agrees on the best features to have in an urban park.

_____

**2.** We need to continue to work together to fight for the preservation of scenic areas and wildlife refuges in our state.

_____

**3.** If you want to see amazing scenery that is different from anywhere else in the country, visit the Grand Canyon.

_____

**4.** Botanical gardens combine beauty and education in a variety of ways.

_____

**Name(s):** _____

# Restating or Explaining

## ➤ Part One

Reread your ideas for writing an opinion paragraph from previous lessons. Think especially about your topic sentence. Practice writing a concluding sentence for a paragraph you might write about your opinion of this topic.

**1.** Write a concluding sentence that restates your opinion.

_____

_____

_____

**2.** Write a concluding sentence that explains why you have this opinion.

_____

_____

_____

**3.** Write a concluding sentence that explains why you wrote that paragraph.

_____

_____

_____

**4.** Which concluding sentence do you think is the most effective? Why?

_____

_____

_____

## ➤ Part Two

Copy your topic sentence onto a piece of paper and exchange papers with a classmate. On the lines below, write a concluding sentence based on your partner's topic sentence.

_____

_____

_____

_____

# First Draft and Peer Review

## ➤ Objective

Students will write the first drafts of their opinion paragraphs and participate in a peer-review activity.

## ➤ Introduction

*Today you will use your writing from previous lessons to write a first draft of an opinion paragraph. You will use the topic and opinion statement from "My Opinion About Parks" (page 13).*

## ➤ Instruction

*A draft is not the finished piece. It is a rough copy, a place where you refer to any notes you have made and write your ideas as sentences and paragraphs. Remember to begin with a topic sentence that includes an opinion; include reasons, facts, and details; and finish with a concluding sentence. Use linking words and phrases to connect your reasons to your opinion. During the drafting process, we revise our writing to make it stronger. In opinion writing, we want to convince our readers to agree with our opinion or take a particular action.*

## ➤ Guided Practice

*After you write your first draft, you will work with a partner to review your writing and improve it. As you read your partner's writing, offer positive and constructive feedback. Everyone likes to hear what they've done right. Begin by telling your partner what you liked about his or her piece. Then suggest one specific way the writing could be made stronger.*

## ➤ Independent Practice

*You will participate in a peer-review activity.* Distribute "Friendly Feedback" (page 23). *This page will help you think about ways you can offer positive feedback and constructive criticism to your partner. Read your partner's opinion piece carefully, then read the suggestions and complete the sentences on the activity page. Discuss your comments.*

## ➤ Review

Prompt students to review the feedback they received from their partners. Discuss with students their takeaway from writing first drafts and having a peer review as part of the writing process.

## ➤ Closing

*Today you wrote a first draft of your opinion piece and reviewed a partner's writing. In the next lesson, you will write a second draft.*

Name(s): _____

# Friendly Feedback

## ➤ Step #1: Give positive feedback

**A.** Consider the following aspects of your partner's writing to identify something you like about his or her writing.

- The author's opinion is clearly stated.
- The topic sentence is clearly related to the topic.
- The piece has reasons that make sense and are related to the topic.
- Interesting facts and details support the reasons.
- Linking words and phrases connect the reasons to the topic sentence.
- Readers are encouraged to change their thinking or behavior.
- The piece motivates readers to take specific action.
- The concluding sentence restates the opinion and main idea in an interesting way.

**B.** Complete one or more of the following sentences. Be prepared to discuss your comment(s).

One thing I like about your opinion piece is _____

_____

_____.

I like how you _____

_____.

You did a good job _____

_____.

## ➤ Step #2: Suggest constructive changes

**A.** Read through the characteristics of strong opinion writing listed above. What is one sentence or particular part of the piece you read that could be changed to make it more effective? Circle the sentence on your partner's draft.

**B.** Complete one of the following sentences. Be prepared to discuss your comment.

One way to make this more effective could be _____

_____

_____.

What if you try _____

_____?

The facts or details explain _____

_____.

# Second Draft and Self-Evaluation

## ➤ Objective

Students will write the second drafts of their opinion paragraphs and conduct a self-evaluation.

## ➤ Introduction

*Today you will refer to your first draft with the suggestions you received from a partner to write a second draft of your opinion paragraph. You will also evaluate your writing.*

## ➤ Instruction

*The drafting part of the writing process happens when we focus on ways to make our writing better. It is also important to correctly use writing conventions, such as capitalization, grammar, punctuation, and spelling. They make our writing easier to read.*

## ➤ Guided Practice

*As you work with your first draft and revise it to write a second draft, focus on specific aspects of opinion writing. Distribute "Evaluating My Writing" (page 25). Use Part One to review the characteristics of effective opinion writing. Then use your second draft to complete the graphic organizer in Part Two. Be sure to polish your draft by checking your paragraph for the errors listed in Part Three. Remember to also incorporate the suggestions you received from your partner during the previous lesson when you write your second draft.*

## ➤ Independent Practice

*When we evaluate something, we look at it carefully to see what is good and valuable in it. Today we will think about how we incorporated aspects of effective opinion writing. It's also important to note areas in which we are still learning and need more practice. Distribute "Self-Evaluation:  Opinion Paragraph" (page 26). This chart shows the characteristics I will look for when I read your opinion paragraphs. Use this page as a guide to help you evaluate your second draft.*

## ➤ Review

Discuss how using a model (e.g., list of characteristics, graphic organizer) aided students in evaluating their writing. Answer any questions about editing to make writing correct.

## ➤ Closing

*Today you wrote a second draft of your opinion piece and evaluated it for effectiveness based on characteristics of strong opinion writing. You also checked your draft for correct writing conventions.*

**Name(s):** _____

# Evaluating My Writing

## ➤ Part One

Read through your first draft and refer to the characteristics listed below to write a second draft.

1. This type of writing <u>states an opinion</u> (or <u>states the author's viewpoint</u>) about a topic.

2. It gives <u>reasons</u> and <u>evidence</u> to <u>support</u> the topic sentence.

3. The concluding sentence may ask <u>readers</u> to <u>change</u> their beliefs or take <u>action</u>.

## ➤ Part Two

Complete the graphic organizer below with information from your second draft. On the arrows, write linking words and phrases from your writing.

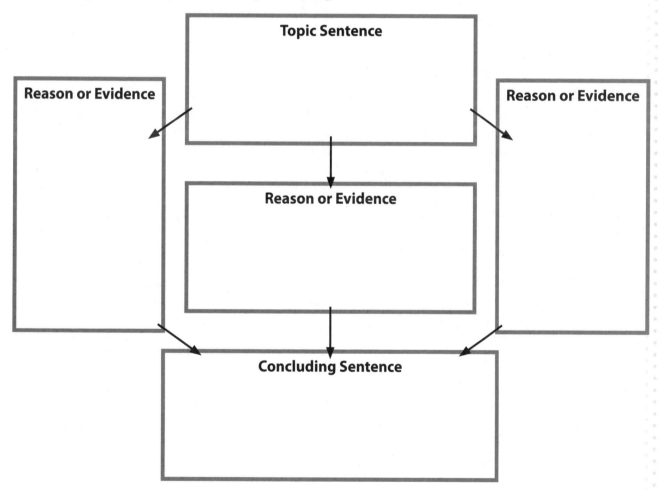

## ➤ Part Three

Use the following checklist to review your writing and correct any errors.

☐ Capitalization      ☐ Grammar      ☐ Punctuation      ☐ Spelling

# Self-Evaluation: Opinion Paragraph

Name: _____    Score: _____

| | 4 | 3 | 2 | 1 |
|---|---|---|---|---|
| **Topic Sentence** | My topic sentence clearly states my opinion about parks and introduces my specific topic in an interesting way. | My topic sentence states my opinion and is related to my topic. | My topic sentence states an opinion. | My topic sentence does not state an opinion and/or is not related to the topic. |
| **Organization** | I organized my paragraph with related ideas grouped together to explain why I hold this opinion about parks. | I grouped some related ideas to support my opinion about parks. | My ideas support my opinion, but they are not organized in any particular order. | My ideas do not support or explain my opinion in a way that would convince readers. |
| **Reasons and Evidence** | My paragraph includes reasons that clearly support my opinion about parks with relevant evidence, including facts and details. | My paragraph includes reasons that support my opinion about parks with some facts and details. | My paragraph includes reasons and a few details about parks. | My reasons are not related to my opinion or the topic of parks and do not include details. |
| **Linking Words** | My opinion and supporting reasons are connected in a logical way with appropriate linking words and phrases. | My opinion and supporting reasons are connected with linking words and phrases. | Some of my reasons are connected to my opinion with linking words and phrases. | My reasons are not connected in any way to my opinion. |
| **Concluding Sentence** | My paragraph has a concluding sentence that is directly related to my opinion about parks and challenges the reader to change the way they think or behave. | My paragraph has a concluding sentence that is related to my opinion about parks and considers the reader. | My paragraph has a concluding sentence that is related to my opinion or says something about parks. | My concluding sentence is not related to my opinion and is not about parks. |

# Final Draft

## ➤ Objective

Students will consider their audience and write final drafts of their opinion paragraphs.

## ➤ Introduction

*Most writing is meant to be shared with an audience, either read aloud or in some printed form. Today you will think about who would be most interested in your opinion paragraph and write a final draft for publication.*

## ➤ Instruction

*A final draft is the finished piece that we will share with others. You may have heard this referred to as "publishing." Publishing includes the idea that the work will be made available to others in some format.*

## ➤ Guided Practice

*Think about the opinion piece you have been writing—your topic sentence, reasons for your opinion, and concluding sentence to convince readers to change the way they think or take a particular action. Who might be interested in this topic? What would be the best way to share your opinion with your audience?* Discuss with students possible ways to publish their writing.

## ➤ Independent Practice

Distribute "Publish a Final Draft" (page 28). *You will identify an appropriate audience for your writing and write a plan to publish your writing. Your plan might include reading your work aloud, presenting a final copy to a particular person, including your writing in a newsletter, or posting it on a classroom blog. You will then write a final draft of your opinion paragraph. Remember to incorporate any corrections you made to the second draft as well as revisions that strengthen your writing and make it more effective.*

## ➤ Review

Review the concept of publication: students will generate a final copy of their writing to share with others by reading aloud and/or distributing one or more printed copies.

## ➤ Closing

*Today you wrote a final draft of your opinion paragraph and made a plan to "publish" (share) it with a specific audience.*

Name(s): _____

# Publish a Final Draft

## ➤ Step #1: Identify your audience

**A.** Picture an auditorium. In the "stage" box, write the title of your opinion piece. In the "seat" circles, write (by name or category) those who might be in your audience (e.g., friends, family, classmates, people in the school or community).

**B.** Write a one- or two-sentence plan for publishing your writing for your audience.

_____

_____

_____

_____

_____

## ➤ Step #2: Write a final draft

Refer to your second draft and the revisions, including corrections, you have made. Write a final copy of your opinion paragraph on a separate piece of paper.

# Final Evaluation

## ➤ Objective

Students will compare the teacher's evaluation of their writing with a student evaluation and discuss their observations with a classmate.

## ➤ Introduction

*In a previous lesson, you evaluated your writing using a rubric. Today you will receive the scores I gave your writing using a similar rubric and compare the two evaluations.*

## ➤ Instruction

*A rubric lists the qualities that make writing effective. Increasing levels of quality receive higher scores on a point scale. Reading the descriptions of these levels helps us know how we can improve our writing.* Display "Teacher Evaluation: Opinion Paragraph" (page 30). *How does the rubric correspond to the characteristics of effective opinion writing we've practiced?* Discuss with students.

## ➤ Guided Practice

Distribute copies of "Teacher Evaluation: Opinion Paragraph," students' completed self-evaluations ("Self-Evaluation: Opinion Paragraph" [page 26]), and "Comparing Evaluations" (page 31). *Use the chart at the top of the "Comparing Evaluations" page to compare the scores I gave your writing with the self-evaluation you completed earlier. Then answer questions 2–3.*

## ➤ Independent Practice

*Work with a partner to discuss what you observed when you compared the two evaluations of your writing. Think about what you have learned from participating in this activity and answer questions 4–5.* As time allows, discuss students' observations and reflections together as a class.

## ➤ Review

Review the categories on each scoring rubric and point out how they are the same, only with slightly different wording to reflect the point of view of the person scoring the writing (student and teacher). Answer any questions about the rubric and writing scores students received.

## ➤ Closing

*Today you reviewed the scores you received on your opinion paragraph and compared them with your self-evaluation scores. We discussed our observations and what we learned from using rubrics to evaluate opinion paragraphs.*

# Teacher Evaluation: Opinion Paragraph

**Student Name:** _____   **Score:** _____

| | 4 | 3 | 2 | 1 |
|---|---|---|---|---|
| **Topic Sentence** | The topic sentence clearly states the author's viewpoint and introduces a chosen topic about public parks in an interesting way. | The topic sentence states the author's opinion about the chosen topic. | The topic sentence states an opinion. | The topic sentence does not state an opinion and/or is not related to the topic of public parks. |
| **Organization** | The author creates a logical organizational structure that groups related ideas to support the author's purpose for writing about public parks. | The author groups some related ideas to support the stated opinion about parks. | The author's ideas in the piece support the author's opinion and purpose in writing about parks, but they are not organized in a logical way. | The author's ideas are not grouped in any logical way and do not support the author's purpose in writing about parks. |
| **Reasons and Evidence** | The paragraph includes reasons that clearly support a stated opinion about public parks with relevant evidence, including facts and details. | The paragraph includes reasons that support an opinion about parks with some facts and details. | The paragraph includes reasons and a few details related to an opinion about parks. | The author's reasons do not relate to the stated opinion or topic of public parks and do not include details. |
| **Linking Words** | The author's opinion about public parks and supporting reasons are connected in a logical way with appropriate linking words and phrases. | The author's opinion and supporting reasons are connected with linking words and phrases. | Some reasons are connected to the author's opinion about parks with linking words and phrases. | The author's reasons are not connected in any way to an opinion about parks. |
| **Concluding Sentence** | The paragraph has a concluding sentence that is directly related to an opinion about public parks and challenges the reader to change his or her thinking or behavior. | The paragraph has a concluding sentence that is related to an opinion about public parks and considers the reader. | The paragraph has a concluding sentence that is related to the author's opinion or the topic of public parks. | The paragraph has a concluding sentence that is not related to the author's opinion or the topic of public parks and has no relevance for the reader. |

**Name(s):** _____

# Comparing Evaluations

Use "Self-Evaluation: Opinion Paragraph" (page 26) and "Teacher Evaluation: Opinion Paragraph" (page 30) to compare your evaluation of your writing with your teacher's assessment. Then discuss your answers with a partner.

1.  Use the scores from the self-evaluation to complete the "Student" column of the chart. Then use the scores from the teacher evaluation to complete the "Teacher" column of the chart.

| | Student | Teacher |
|---|---|---|
| Topic Sentence | | |
| Organization | | |
| Reasons and Evidence | | |
| Linking Words | | |
| Concluding Sentence | | |
| **Total Score** | | |

2.  In which areas are your scores higher than the scores you received from your teacher? Why do you think the scores differ?

    _____

    _____

    _____

3.  In which areas did you receive scores from your teacher that are higher than those you gave yourself? Why do you think the scores differ?

    _____

    _____

    _____

4.  Which total score do you think best reflects the overall effectiveness of your writing? Why?

    _____

    _____

    _____

5.  What do these scores show you about ways in which you can improve your writing?

    _____

    _____

    _____

# Review

## ➤ Objective

Students will read opinion paragraphs and identify the topic sentence, reasons, linking words, and concluding sentence in each paragraph.

## ➤ Introduction

*Today we will review what makes opinion writing effective by reading opinion paragraphs and identifying elements within each paragraph. You will explain how you know and recognize each part.*

## ➤ Instruction

*When we review something, we look at it again. This helps us to remember what we've learned. Opinion writing, by definition, has a clear statement of opinion. It is writing in which an author states a particular point of view about a topic. The author supports the opinion in the topic sentence with related reasons and evidence, such as facts and details. A concluding sentence restates the topic sentence and convinces the reader to agree or take action.*

## ➤ Guided Practice

Distribute "The Benefits of Botanical Gardens" (page 33). *Work with a partner to identify the topic sentence, reasons, linking words, and concluding sentence in the paragraph. Discuss and defend your answers with your partner. Support your choices with reasons why you identified those sentences as a particular part of opinion writing.*

## ➤ Independent Practice

*Now you will read a paragraph and consider the aspects of opinion writing we've discussed.* Distribute "Exciting Wooden Roller Coasters" (page 34).

## ➤ Review

Review students' work from "Exciting Wooden Roller Coasters" and discuss reasons students identified particular phrases and sentences the way they did.

## ➤ Closing

*We have spent several days examining how to write opinion paragraphs. You have written your own opinion pieces to share with a specific audience.*

## ➤ Answers

"The Benefits of Botanical Gardens" (page 33): 1. *topic sentence:* A botanical garden would be valuable for our community; *reasons (paraphrased):* People would learn about different kinds of plants that grow naturally in this area. Visitors would learn how plants grow and their uses. The money could be used to develop public parks; *linking words:* especially, in order, in addition; *concluding sentence:* A botanical garden would help us learn about plants and their benefits in our local environment.

"Exciting Wooden Roller Coasters" (page 34): 1. Every amusement park should have at least one wooden roller coaster. *topic:* wooden roller coasters; 2. suspense, feeling of speed, doesn't go upside down, beautiful scenery; 3. In my opinion, another reason; 4. The next time you're at an amusement park, try a ride on a roller coaster.

Name(s): _____

# The Benefits of Botanical Gardens

Read the paragraph and then complete the activity below.

A botanical garden would be valuable for our community. This type of garden has different kinds of plants, especially those that grow naturally in this area. People could read labels describing each plant in order to learn how the plant grows and its uses. In addition, a small fee might be charged for admission to the garden. The money could be used to develop other kinds of public parks in the neighborhood. These gardens provide a place to study and preserve rare plants. A botanical garden would help us learn about plants and their benefits in our local environment.

1. Mark each part of the opinion paragraph.
   - Underline the topic sentence.
   - Draw boxes around the reasons.
   - Circle the linking words.
   - Draw a wavy line under the concluding sentence.

2. Write notes to explain why you chose to mark each phrase or sentence the way you did. Refer to activities from earlier lessons (such as "Understanding Opinion Writing" [page 6] or "Evaluating My Writing" [page 25]) if needed.

   _____

   _____

   _____

   _____

3. Listen as your partner reads and explains his or her answers. Confirm your partner's markings with a thumbs-up/thumbs-down signal.

4. Discuss with your partner how you marked each part of the paragraph. Use your notes above to justify your choices.

---

### Teacher Notes

Grade level: appropriate
Lexile estimate: 940L

---

**Name(s):** _____

# Exciting Wooden Roller Coasters

Read the paragraph and then complete the activity below.

Every amusement park should have at least one wooden roller coaster. Roller coaster fans call these rides "woodies." The tracks often don't go as high as steel coasters. In my opinion, the slow pull of the chain up the hill creates awesome suspense. As the train crests the hill into the first drop, the track shakes just enough to make it feel as though you're going very fast. Another reason I like these coasters is they can have fantastic twists and turns that increase momentum. This type of roller coaster might not be as likely to go upside down. That's okay with me! Some wooden roller coasters travel through beautiful scenery, adding enjoyment to the ride. The next time you're at an amusement park, try a ride on a wooden roller coaster. It's a great experience!

1. Underline the topic sentence. Based on this sentence, what is the author's opinion? What is the topic of the paragraph?

   _____

   _____

2. What reasons does the author give for having this opinion?

   _____

   _____

3. Which words or phrases link the reasons to the topic sentence?

   _____

   _____

4. Highlight the concluding sentence. What change in thinking or call to action does the author ask readers to make?

   _____

   _____

5. What is your opinion about the topic of this paragraph?

   _____

   _____

---

**Teacher Notes**

Grade level: appropriate

Lexile estimate: 880L

---

# Introductory Paragraphs

## ➤ Objective

Students will brainstorm in small groups and individually and then participate in a "quick write" to generate opinions, ideas, and reasons about a topic related to transportation technology.

## ➤ Introduction

*You have learned how to write an effective opinion paragraph. Today we will discuss the opening, or introductory, paragraph of an opinion essay. The topic for this module is new transportation technology.*

## ➤ Instruction

*An opinion paragraph has a stated opinion, usually in the first sentence. In an opinion essay, the topic sentence is also called the thesis statement. The thesis statement is given in an opening paragraph, but it may or may not be the first sentence. This first paragraph introduces the topic and summarizes the reasons for the opinion.*

## ➤ Guided Practice

*What is a key feature of an effective opinion paragraph?* (The thesis statement clearly states an opinion.) *Many people have definite opinions about the environment. Transportation is a human endeavor that affects the environment.* Briefly discuss and introduce general concepts and topics of transportation technology with the class. *With a small group, you will think of possible opinions people might hold for or against a particular type of transportation technology and their reasons for having that opinion.* Distribute "Let's Discuss Transportation" (page 36).

## ➤ Independent Practice

*Think about the topics mentioned in the class discussion and your small group.* Distribute "My Ideas About Transportation Technology" (page 37). *Write a topic that particularly interests you at the top of the graphic organizer. As you brainstorm, add reasons to support your opinion(s) about your topic and arguments for or against your position. Write key words and ideas as you think about your selected topic.*

*Refer to your brainstorming notes to "quick write" a journal entry.* Distribute "Moving in a Forward Direction" (page 38). If desired, set a timer for students or refer them to a start and finish time on a clock. *Do not stop to edit your thoughts or make changes as you write. Write anything that comes to mind about your topic idea.*

## ➤ Review

Review student notes from the three brainstorming sessions and elicit from students sample thesis statements about the topic.

## ➤ Closing

*Today you brainstormed opinions and ideas to think about how you will introduce a selected topic.*

**Name(s):** _____

# Let's Discuss Transportation

## ➤ Part One

Discuss with your group an aspect of transportation/transportation technology (e.g., hybrid or autonomous vehicles) that might be the topic for an opinion essay. Use the following prompts as discussion starters:

- Which new transportation technology should receive the most resources and development?
- Which transportation technology is beneficial to the environment?
- Which transportation technology is harmful to the environment?
- Why are people interested in autonomous cars?
- Which new transportation technology would you most like to see developed?

## ➤ Part Two

As a group, draft a statement for and against this type of transportation/transportation technology. Write each statement in the appropriate column in the chart below. Then write reasons people might hold an opinion for or against this type of transportation/transportation technology.

| For | Against |
|---|---|
|  |  |
| **Reasons** | **Reasons** |
|  |  |

**Name(s):** _____

# My Ideas About Transportation Technology

Use the graphic organizer below to brainstorm your ideas about transportation/transportation technology. Write a topic idea in the top box and take notes about anything that comes to mind about that topic. Refer to your notes from the small-group discussion in "Let's Discuss Transportation" (page 36) for ideas. Partway through the process, you may realize you are mostly against a particular idea or do not have much to say about it. That's okay. Write reasons people might be against your opinion. Then go back to other ideas you have about the topic and brainstorm some more.

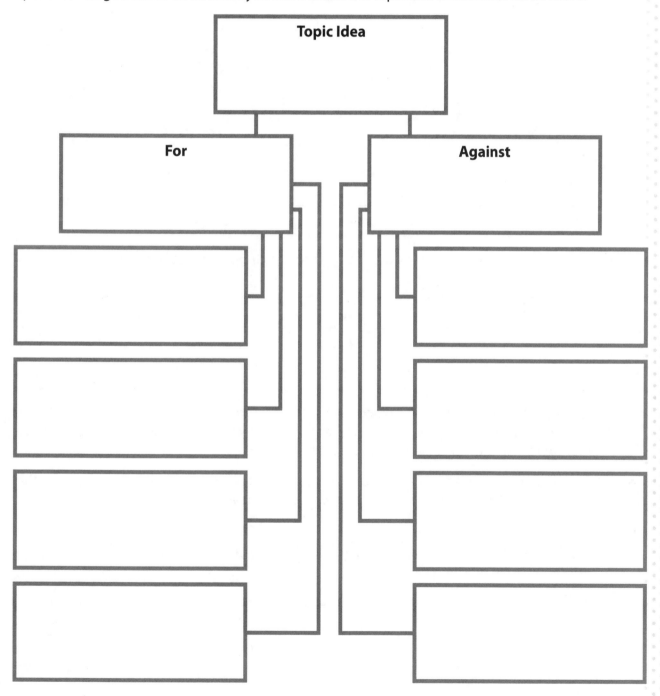

Name(s): _____

# Moving in a Forward Direction

Complete this activity in order to develop your thesis statement on transportation technology.

**1.** What topic will you write about?

_____

_____

_____

**2.** Remember that a thesis statement clearly states an opinion about a topic. What is your opinion about the topic you selected? Use the suggested words below to help you state an opinion.

| believe | claim | feel | think |

_____

_____

_____

**3.** Write a thesis statement that includes the topic and your opinion about the topic.

_____

_____

_____

_____

**4.** Keep your thesis statement in mind and write for 10 minutes without stopping to reread your work. Follow the direction your thoughts take you, even if you stray and explore another aspect of your topic. Use the back of this page to write.

**5.** At the end of your writing time, look back over your "quick write." Underline any sentences that strongly relate to your topic that you might want to use in your essay. Circle reasons, facts, and feelings that jump out as expressions of your opinion.

**6.** Write any further notes you want to remember when you get ready to write an introductory paragraph for your opinion essay.

_____

_____

_____

_____

_____

# Body Paragraphs

## ➤ Objective

Students will brainstorm evidence and reasons that support their opinions from the previous lesson, compare their arguments with partners, and take notes to strengthen their reasons.

## ➤ Introduction

*Today you will complete a graphic organizer to think about the reasons and evidence you will use to support your opinion about transportation technology. You will compare arguments and reflect on your discussion to strengthen your body paragraphs.*

## ➤ Instruction

*Each paragraph in the body of your essay explains and supports one of the reasons introduced in the opening paragraph. These paragraphs contain the facts and details that relate to the reasons. Include examples to show readers why your opinion is valid. Linking words and phrases will help readers understand the connections between reasons and the topic sentence.*

## ➤ Guided Practice

*Which topic did you choose for your opinion essay?* Distribute "Reasons and Evidence" (page 40). Hand out index cards or allow time for students to cut pieces of paper. *Refer to your notes from the previous lesson to write your thesis statement on a card. Set that card aside. List reasons for your opinion on the cards, with one reason on each card. Below the reason (or on the back of the card), write examples, facts, details, and other evidence that would convince readers to agree with your thinking. Arrange the reason cards in an order that makes sense. Read through the evidence listed for each reason and determine if it is most closely related to that reason. If the evidence fits better with another reason, change your notes. Use your note cards to complete the graphic organizer.*

## ➤ Independent Practice

Distribute "Comparing Arguments" (page 41). *First, you will write a paragraph to explain and provide evidence for one of the reasons you listed in "Reasons and Evidence." Then you will work with a partner who wrote from a different perspective or opposing viewpoint.*

## ➤ Review

Review examples of student graphic organizers to discuss how writers use examples, facts, and details as reasons to support a thesis statement. Help students clarify and refine their reasons as needed.

## ➤ Closing

*Today you thought about reasons that support your thesis statement about transportation technology. You compared your opinion with a partner's opinion to strengthen your argument.*

**Name(s):** _____

# Reasons and Evidence

Complete this activity using index cards or small pieces of paper.

1.  Write your thesis statement on a card. Set that card aside.

2.  List reasons for your opinion on cards, with one reason on each card. Below the reason (or on the back of the card), write related examples, facts, details, and other evidence to convince readers to agree with your thinking.

3.  Arrange the reason cards in an order that makes sense. Read through the evidence listed for each reason and determine how closely it relates to that reason. If the evidence fits better with another reason, change your notes.

4.  Copy the final order of your reasons and evidence in the graphic organizer below.

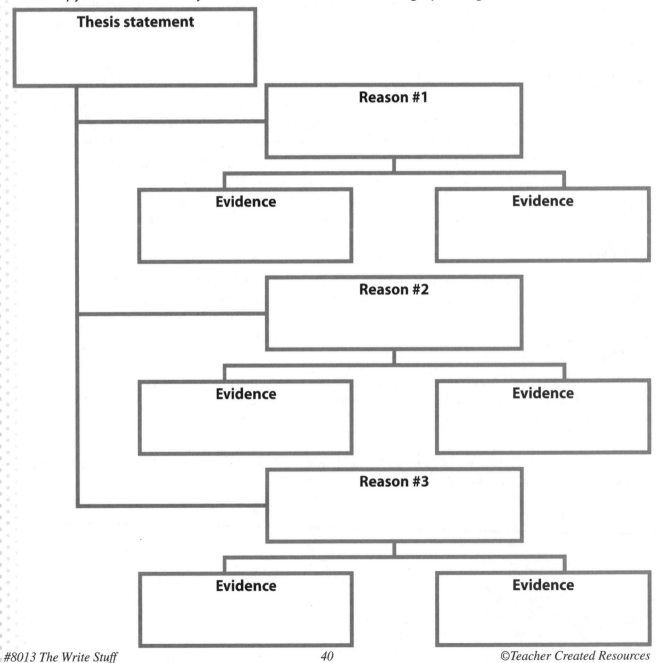

**Name(s):** _____

# Comparing Arguments

## ➤ Part One

On a separate piece of paper, write a paragraph to explain and provide evidence to support one of your reasons.

## ➤ Part Two

Work with a partner to compare and contrast your opinions about transportation technology. Read each other's arguments and complete the Venn diagram.

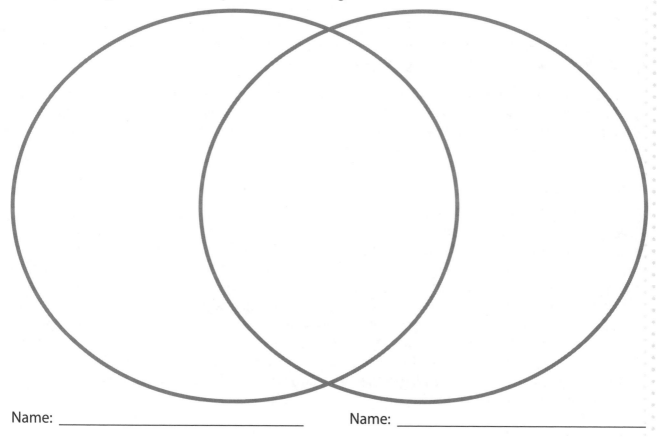

Name: _____        Name: _____

## ➤ Part Three

1.  On a separate piece of paper, write a paragraph discussing what you observed about the similarities and differences of opinion between you and your partner.

2.  What strengths and weaknesses did you notice in your argument? How well do your reasons support your opinion? On the "Reasons and Evidence" chart (page 40), add notes about how you might strengthen your reasons.

_____

_____

_____

_____

# Concluding Paragraphs

## ➤ Objective

Students will work together as a class to generate sample concluding paragraphs based on a given thesis statement and will choose one model to practice writing a concluding paragraph related to the opinion they stated in their introductory paragraph thesis statement.

## ➤ Introduction

*Now that we've thought about the introductory and body paragraphs of an opinion essay, we'll address the concluding paragraph.*

## ➤ Instruction

*The concluding paragraph restates the opinion. It summarizes the reasons why the author holds that opinion. It may ask readers to change their way of thinking or take action.*

*Concluding paragraphs may follow one of several different formats. A summary provides readers with an overview of the topic and the reasons for the author's opinion. A concluding paragraph may prompt readers to think more about the issue. Authors may conclude by encouraging readers to take action. The concluding paragraph of an opinion essay may also try to convince readers to agree with the stated opinion.*

## ➤ Guided Practice

Display "The Right Conclusion" (page 43) and introduce the four types of concluding paragraphs, clarifying that each model also includes a restatement of the topic and author's opinion, along with a summary of the author's reasons for the opinion. Then read aloud the thesis statement on "The Right Conclusion." Divide students into small groups, making sure each group is assigned a model and all four models are represented. *Answer question 1, restating the thesis statement as a concluding sentence that includes an opinion. Work with your group to write a sample concluding paragraph based on the thesis statement. Follow your assigned model. Then answer questions 2 and 3.* Prompt groups to share their samples with the class and discuss each type of concluding paragraph. *What linking words could we use to let readers know this is the author's conclusion on the issue?* Prompt students to write sample sentences using possible linking words (all things considered, therefore, in conclusion, for these reasons, as a result of, altogether, overall, consequently). *Add one or more linking words, as appropriate, to at least one of the displayed sample paragraphs.*

## ➤ Independent Practice

Distribute "Practice Writing a Concluding Paragraph" (page 44). *Choose one model presented in the class activity. Imitate the model to write a sample concluding paragraph based on your thesis statement and supporting reasons.*

## ➤ Review

Review the different approaches to writing a concluding paragraph. Prompt students to evaluate which approach might be best for their thesis statements and opinion essays.

## ➤ Closing

*We practiced writing sample concluding paragraphs together as a class. You then imitated one of the models to write a sample concluding paragraph based on your opinion about transportation technology.*

# The Right Conclusion

Follow along as the class discusses different types of concluding paragraphs for an opinion essay.

| Summarize | Consider the Issue |
|---|---|
| Provide readers with an overview of the topic and reasons for the author's opinion. | Prompt readers to think more deeply about the topic with suggested actions or a summary of reasons. |
| **Take Action** | **Convince Readers to Agree** |
| Encourage readers to do something as a result of the opinion and reasons presented. | Include persuasive statements and reasons to convince readers to agree with the author. |

*Thesis statement:* Personal cars are not the answer for everyone.

1. With a group, restate the thesis statement above as a concluding sentence with an opinion. Then continue to finish the concluding paragraph.

_____
_____
_____
_____
_____
_____
_____
_____

2. Which model did your group use when writing your practice concluding paragraph? In what ways was your model effective or ineffective for the thesis statement?

_____
_____
_____
_____

3. What would you change in your group's sample concluding paragraph to strengthen it?

_____
_____
_____

**Name(s):** _____

# Practice Writing a Concluding Paragraph

## ➤ Part One

Choose one model (Summarize, Consider the Issue, Take Action, or Convince Readers to Agree) that was presented in "The Right Conclusion" (page 43) to complete the following activity.

1. Which model will you follow to write a sample concluding paragraph that relates to the topic and opinion in your introductory paragraph? Why?

   _____

   _____

   _____

   _____

   _____

2. What will you need to include for your concluding paragraph to be effective?

   _____

   _____

   _____

   _____

   _____

## ➤ Part Two

Imitate the model you chose in Part One to write a sample concluding paragraph based on your thesis statement, opinion, and supporting reasons about transportation technology. Refer to "Reasons and Evidence" (page 40) to help you as you practice writing your concluding paragraph.

_____

_____

_____

_____

_____

_____

_____

_____

Underline or highlight specific phrases and sentences that indicate which model you followed.

# First Draft and Peer Review

## ➤ Objective

Students will participate in a peer-review activity to strengthen their opinion essay arguments and then write first drafts of their essays.

## ➤ Introduction

*Today you will discuss your opinions with a partner and consider different perspectives, reasons, and arguments related to your essay topic. You will also write a first draft of an opinion essay.*

## ➤ Instruction

*A draft of an opinion essay will include all the parts you've worked on so far. Your draft will include an introductory paragraph. Body paragraphs will explain and support your reasons with evidence such as facts and details. Often, an opinion essay will address an opposing viewpoint to the stated opinion. This shows readers how the author's opinion is valid and worthy of readers' consideration, belief, or action.*

## ➤ Guided Practice

*Understanding how someone else thinks about an issue enables us to write a stronger opinion essay. When we share different viewpoints, we clarify why we hold a certain opinion and get ideas for how to address an opposing argument in an opinion essay. Write your thesis statement from "Moving in a Forward Direction" (page 38) and discuss it with a partner.* Distribute "Opposing Viewpoints" (page 46) and pair students with partners who may have opposing views, if possible. *Take notes to complete the chart for your opinion. Allow time to discuss your partner's opinion statement in the same way. After you write your first draft, review your writing with a different partner using the rubric in Part Two of the "Opposing Viewpoints" page.*

## ➤ Independent Practice

*Refer to your notes and writing samples from previous lessons to write a first draft of your opinion essay. Remember to write one body paragraph to explain and support each reason for your thesis statement. Each paragraph should have its own topic sentence related to the reason discussed. Include linking words to connect reasons to the stated opinion. Evaluate the effectiveness of the sample concluding paragraph you wrote in the previous lesson and modify as necessary.*

## ➤ Review

Review students' notes on opposing viewpoints for their opinions as needed to help them see both sides of an argument. Discuss together as a class as time allows. Review the rubric for peer review and discussion and answer any questions.

## ➤ Closing

*You have strengthened the reasons and arguments for your stated opinion by hearing other viewpoints on the topic and have written a first draft of your opinion essay.*

**Name(s):** _____

# Opposing Viewpoints

## ➤ Part One

**1.** Write your thesis statement about transportation technology.

_____

_____

_____

**2.** Work with a partner to complete the chart below.

| I think . . . | My partner thinks . . . |
|---|---|
| | |

**3.** Based on your discussion with your partner, what opposing argument or reasons could you address in one of your body paragraphs?

_____

_____

## ➤ Part Two

Work with a different partner to review each other's drafts and provide feedback. Use the simple rubric below as a guide and discussion starter. Make a checkmark in the appropriate box.

| | You're an expert! | Good work! | Needs polishing |
|---|---|---|---|
| The introductory paragraph clearly states an opinion and introduces the reasons that will be discussed. | | | |
| Each body paragraph gives support and evidence for one reason. | | | |
| The concluding paragraph restates the thesis statement, summarizes the reasons for the author's opinion, and engages the reader in some way. | | | |

# Second Draft and Self-Evaluation

## ➤ Objective

Students will write second drafts of their opinion essays and participate in a self-evaluation activity.

## ➤ Introduction

*Today you will write the second draft of your essay, use a rubric to evaluate your writing, and discuss the evaluation process with a partner.*

## ➤ Instruction

*In the previous lesson, you worked with a partner to review your first draft. You should have notes about things you want to change to make your writing more effective. What is the overall goal in an opinion essay?* (to convince readers to change the way they think or behave) *Even though you have already written a rough copy of your essay, this is not your final draft. You will make more changes to this second draft.*

## ➤ Guided Practice

*Reread each paragraph of your first draft and think about the writing activities you have done to generate ideas for that section of the essay. As you read, ask yourself, "What is the purpose of this part? Will readers understand what I am trying to say here?" Then go back and check to make sure it all makes sense. Are the body paragraphs in a logical order with each paragraph focused on one reason and its supporting evidence? Read your concluding paragraph and make sure it restates your opinion and summarizes the reasons for that opinion in a convincing way. Use your notes to write a second draft of your opinion essay on transportation technology.*

## ➤ Independent Practice

Distribute "Self-Evaluation:  Opinion Essay" (page 48). *Evaluate your second draft using the rubric as a guide. Then discuss your observations about each aspect of your opinion essay with a partner. On which parts of your essay did you score the highest? How do these areas represent improvement over your opinion paragraph from Module 1? In which areas of your essay do you still see a need for improvement? What specifically would you like to work on doing better?*

*Discuss how it feels to evaluate your own writing. What are the hardest and easiest parts of the process for you?*

## ➤ Review

Review the rubric with students and answer any questions about how they will score their second drafts and discuss the process with a partner.

## ➤ Closing

*Use your self-evaluation and discussion notes from reviewing your second draft with your partner to write a final draft of your opinion essay. Bring your final copy back to class for the next lesson.*

# Self-Evaluation: Opinion Essay

Name: _____     Score: _____

| | 4 | 3 | 2 | 1 |
|---|---|---|---|---|
| **Introductory Paragraph** | My introductory paragraph has a thesis statement that clearly states my opinion about an aspect of transportation technology and introduces related reasons. | My introductory paragraph has a thesis statement that states my opinion about transportation and introduces my reasons. | My introductory paragraph includes an opinion I have about transportation. | My introductory paragraph does not state an opinion about transportation and/or does not introduce any reasons. |
| **Body Paragraphs** | Each body paragraph explains and presents relevant evidence, such as facts and details, for one reason that supports my thesis statement about transportation technology. | Each body paragraph includes a reason that supports my thesis statement about transportation technology with some facts and details. | Each body paragraph includes a reason and a few details about transportation. | My reasons are not related to my thesis statement or the transportation topic introduced in the opening paragraph and do not include details. |
| **Organization** | My introductory paragraph and body paragraphs are organized in a logical way, and I use appropriate linking words and phrases. | My introductory paragraph and body paragraphs are organized, and I use some linking words and phrases. | Some of my body paragraphs are organized, but I do not use linking words and phrases. | My body paragraphs are not organized in a way that makes sense. |
| **Concluding Paragraph** | My essay has an effective concluding paragraph that is directly related to my thesis statement about transportation technology and considers the reader's response. | My essay has a concluding paragraph that is related to my thesis statement about transportation technology and considers the reader's response. | My essay has a concluding paragraph that is related to my thesis statement or says something about transportation. | My concluding paragraph is not related to my thesis statement and is not about transportation. |

# Review

## ➤ Objective

Students will use what they have learned about the structure of an opinion essay to correctly arrange sentences from one sample essay and evaluate another sample essay.

## ➤ Introduction

*Today we will review writing an opinion essay. We will think about the characteristics of an effective opinion essay.*

## ➤ Instruction

*Let's think about what we have learned about writing an opinion essay.* Discuss. *The introductory paragraph contains a thesis statement and an overview of reasons that support the author's opinion. Each body paragraph presents evidence, including facts and details, to support one reason. Body paragraphs should be in a logical order that relates to the overview in the introductory paragraph. A separate body paragraph may address an opposing argument. A concluding paragraph restates the opinion and summarizes the reasons for that opinion.*

## ➤ Guided Practice

Display paragraphs from "Hybrid Vehicles" (page 50) out of order. Work together as a class to rewrite or arrange the paragraphs in correct order. *How can what you know about thesis statements, opinions, introductory paragraphs, body paragraphs, and concluding sentences help us reconstruct this essay correctly?*

## ➤ Independent Practice

Distribute "Vehicles Without Drivers" (page 51). *As you read this essay, think about what makes it effective opinion writing. Then answer the questions.* As time allows, have students share their responses with partners.

## ➤ Review

Review student responses for the Independent Practice activity. Clarify any misunderstandings.

## ➤ Closing

*You have read two opinion essays to review the characteristics of effective opinion writing. Each essay had a topic sentence, reasons and evidence, and a concluding paragraph.*

## ➤ Teacher Note

Collect students' essays and grade them using "Teacher Evaluation: Opinion Essay" (page 54).

## ➤ Answers

"Vehicles Without Drivers" (page 51): 1. Our society needs a solution for distracted driving, and autonomous vehicles might be the answer; 2. Autonomous vehicles do not have drivers, people are distracted when they drive, distracted driving is a safety concern, autonomous vehicles will make driving safer; 3. Accidents can still happen.

# Hybrid Vehicles

Hybrid vehicles have become more popular in recent years. They do not use as much conventional gasoline, which reduces dependency on foreign oil. Since they run partially on electricity or battery power, these vehicles have a lower overall fuel cost. Also, their output of harmful emissions is much lower. As an alternative fuel source, this technology has addressed transportation energy concerns.

The United States gets some of its gasoline from other countries. Changes in supply and price are out of our country's control. It is wise to produce some of what we need in our own country, and this saves shipping costs, too.

Hybrid vehicles switch back and forth between a gasoline and a battery-powered or electric engine. Therefore, they get higher gas mileage because they do not use as much gas. People who drive these vehicles do not spend as much money on gas.

Electricity is a clean source of fuel. When a vehicle is running on the electric motor, there are no harmful emissions. Some of our electricity is now produced from renewable sources. In this way, this type of vehicle can be good for the environment.

There are some concerns with this technology, though. Oil may be used to produce the batteries and other components of the vehicle. The electricity used to run the car is stored in batteries. The batteries last several years, but they do not last forever. Storage for worn-out batteries is a big problem.

Costs for hybrid vehicles have come down in recent years. This, along with reduced fuel costs, makes them an economical alternative for some people. More places have charging stations now, so they can run more on electricity and save fuel. For now, hybrid vehicles are a reasonable form of energy-efficient transportation.

## Teacher Notes

Grade level: appropriate
Lexile estimate: 890L

**Name(s):** _____

# Vehicles Without Drivers

Our society needs a solution for distracted driving, and autonomous vehicles might be the answer. This type of vehicle runs on "auto pilot." The driver does not play as great a role, so distracted driving is not as much of a safety concern. Automakers are developing autonomous technology to make driving safer for everyone.

Distracted driving has become a safety problem in some cities. People want to save time, so they try to do something else while driving. They may think driving is boring, or they may be running late. People do things that take their attention from the road. This presents a safety hazard, as they find it hard to stay in their lane or follow curves in the road. They don't see stop signals or other vehicles.

Autonomous vehicles do not require as much driver control. The best example of this is a people-mover system at an airport. These automated pods are used as shuttles to transport people from one terminal to another. Since no one actually drives the vehicle, distracted driving is not an issue.

We do not yet have cars that require no driver control. New cars have automated safety features that help drivers, though. A backup camera enables drivers to see obstacles in blind spots. Sensors on some models warn drivers if they drift from their lanes.

These new safety features are not foolproof, though. Accidents can still happen. If used correctly, safety features and automated computer systems in cars do provide some benefits to drivers. Fully automated vehicle technology will not be available for years. The best solution, though, is still to pay attention to the road!

Answer the questions below based on the essay you read. If needed, use the back of this page to write your responses.

1. Restate the author's opinion in your own words.

   _____

2. Based on the introductory paragraph, what reasons for the opinion might the author discuss in the essay?

   _____

3. What opposing argument does the author address?

   _____

4. Write a concluding sentence that restates the thesis statement.

   _____

---

### Teacher Notes

Grade level:  appropriate
Lexile estimate:  870L

---

# Final Evaluation

## ➤ Objective

Students will compare the scores they received on their essays with their self-evaluations.

## ➤ Introduction

*Today you will review your self-evaluation scores, predict the scores you will receive from me, and compare the actual scores to reflect on the effectiveness of your opinion essay.*

## ➤ Instruction

*You evaluated your second draft using the "Self-Evaluation:  Opinion Essay" (page 48). This showed you characteristics of effective opinion writing I would consider when scoring your essays. The rubric gave you information to think about as you wrote your final essay. I have used a very similar rubric to score your opinion essay.*

## ➤ Guided Practice

Distribute students' "Self-Evaluation:  Opinion Essay." *Look at how you scored your essay in each area. In which areas did you think you did well? Which area had the lowest score, showing where you think you could improve?* Distribute "Evaluating My Opinion Essay" (page 53). *Refer to your self-evaluation and your final essay to predict the scores I gave your essay. Discuss your predictions with a partner.*

## ➤ Independent Practice

Distribute "Teacher Evaluation:  Opinion Essay" (page 54) with scored student essays. *Review the evaluation I gave your essay and compare the scores with those on your self-evaluation. Complete Part Two.*

## ➤ Review

Answer any questions students have about teacher evaluation scores. Discuss the role rubrics have in helping students evaluate their writing with the goal of making it more effective. *How does spending time with rubrics help you think about how to make your writing more effective?*

## ➤ Closing

*Reviewing your self-evaluation, predicting the scores you would receive from me, discussing your predictions, and comparing both scores gave you the opportunity to consider different perspectives on your writing.*

Name(s): _____

# Evaluating My Opinion Essay

## ➤ Part One

Think about your final draft and refer to your completed "Self-Evaluation: Opinion Essay" (page 48).

1.  What score do you think you will receive from the teacher in each area?  Highlight or circle the score you think you will receive for each part of your essay.

2.  What are your reasons for each score you predicted?

    _____

    _____

    _____

3.  Share your predictions with a partner and explain your reasoning.

## ➤ Part Two

Review the scores you received for your writing on the "Teacher Evaluation: Opinion Essay" (page 54). Compare these scores with those from your self-evaluation.

1.  How close were your predictions? _____

2.  In which areas were they the closest? _____

3.  In which areas did they differ? _____

    _____

4.  Why do you think the teacher's scores were higher/lower?

    _____

    _____

    _____

5.  What did comparing the scores show you about the effectiveness of your opinion writing?

    _____

    _____

    _____

6.  Which area would you like to work on improving first? Why?

    _____

    _____

    _____

# Teacher Evaluation:  Opinion Essay

**Student Name:** _____     **Score:** _____

|  | 4 | 3 | 2 | 1 |
|---|---|---|---|---|
| **Introductory Paragraph** | The introductory paragraph has a thesis statement that clearly states an opinion about an aspect of transportation technology and introduces related reasons. | The thesis statement states an opinion about transportation and introduces reasons. | The introductory paragraph states an opinion about transportation. | The introductory paragraph does not state an opinion about transportation and/or does not introduce any reasons. |
| **Body Paragraphs** | Each body paragraph explains and presents relevant evidence, such as facts and details, for one reason that supports the author's thesis statement about transportation technology. | Each body paragraph includes a reason that supports the author's thesis statement about transportation technology with some facts and details. | Each body paragraph includes a reason and a few details about transportation. | Reasons are not related to the thesis statement or the transportation topic introduced in the opening paragraph and do not include details. |
| **Organization** | The introductory paragraph and body paragraphs are organized in a logical way, and the author uses appropriate linking words and phrases. | The introductory paragraph and body paragraphs are organized, and the author uses some linking words and phrases. | Some of the body paragraphs are organized, but the author does not use linking words and phrases. | The body paragraphs are not organized in a way that makes sense. |
| **Concluding Paragraph** | The concluding paragraph is effective and is directly related to the thesis statement about transportation technology and considers the reader's response. | The concluding paragraph is related to the thesis statement about transportation technology and considers the reader's response. | The concluding paragraph is related to the thesis statement or says something about transportation. | The concluding paragraph is not related to the thesis statement and is not about transportation. |

# All About Informative/Explanatory Writing

## ➤ Objective

Students will identify characteristics of an informative paragraph as seen in strong examples and apply their learning to change weak examples to make them more effective.

## ➤ Introduction

*Today you will participate in class and partner discussions to identify characteristics of effective informative paragraphs. Our topic for this module is alternate energy sources.*

## ➤ Instruction

*Informative writing examines a topic to convey ideas and information. Explanatory writing explains how something works or tells readers how to do something. A topic sentence clearly introduces what the paragraph will be about. It explains information clearly so readers can understand the topic. Information is grouped in a way that makes sense. Facts, definitions, details, and examples explain the topic for readers. A concluding sentence relates to the topic and restates the main idea.*

## ➤ Guided Practice

Display "Energy from the Sun" (page 56), covering up the Teacher Notes. Discuss key aspects of the informational paragraph: topic sentence, facts and details, and concluding sentence. *What is this paragraph about? How do you know? Which information helps you better understand the topic? Which sentence restates the main idea?* Display "Solar Power" (page 57), covering up the Teacher Notes. *How is this paragraph different from the first paragraph we read? What is missing? What would you add to this paragraph to improve it?*

Distribute "Informative Paragraphs" (page 58). *Work with a small group to complete the chart and compare the two paragraphs. Then answer the questions with your group. Write your answers on a separate piece of paper.*

## ➤ Independent Practice

Distribute "Wave Energy" (page 59). *Read the paragraph and write what you notice about the paragraph. Take turns sharing one thing from your notes with a classmate.* After a minute or so, prompt students to switch partners. *Find another classmate and share something else from your notes.*

Distribute "Ocean Power" (page 60). *Read this paragraph and write what you notice about it. How well does it match the characteristics of an informative paragraph? What would you change? Rewrite the paragraph. Share your ideas with a partner.*

## ➤ Review

Review student responses to discuss the second set of paragraph examples (strong and weak).

## ➤ Closing

*Today we have discussed the characteristics of an informative paragraph, and you have discussed examples with classmates.*

# Energy from the Sun

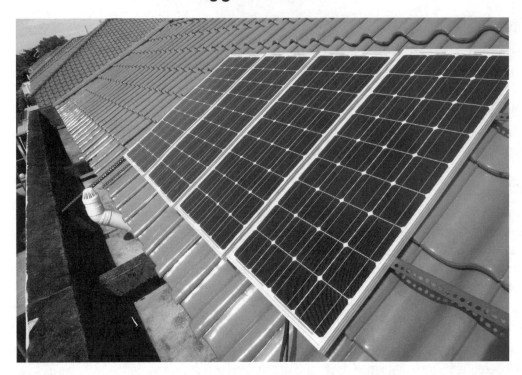

People use energy from the sun for solar power. Solar power is a renewable source of energy. It does not use up Earth's resources or pollute the environment. We use solar power in various ways. Solar panels on the roof of a house convert sunlight into electricity. Some systems use solar power to heat water. People can use the hot water for household uses. Energy from the sun can also heat air. Heating buildings uses a large amount of the total electricity required by a community. Solar power decreases the amount of electricity needed from other sources. Harnessing the sun's energy with solar power provides electricity and benefits the environment at the same time.

---

## Teacher Notes

This is a <u>strong</u> informative paragraph for these reasons:

- The topic sentence clearly states what the paragraph will be about: solar power.
- Information is grouped in a logical way.
- Details and examples explain the topic.
- The concluding sentence summarizes the paragraph and restates the main idea.

> Grade level: appropriate
> Lexile estimate: 770L

# Solar Power

People use solar power in different ways. There are solar panels on the roofs of some houses. If it is cloudy, the panels don't work very well. Some cities have large solar panels next to freeways. Solar energy is sunshine. Other systems use heat energy from the sun to heat or cool water to provide heating and air conditioning for buildings. Solar power saves people money.

---

## Teacher Notes

This is a <u>weak</u> informative paragraph for these reasons:

- The topic sentence states a topic but does not clearly state what the paragraph will be about.
- Information in the paragraph is not arranged in any particular order.
- The facts and examples lack details to explain the information.
- The concluding sentence mentions the topic (solar power) but doesn't relate to the information in the rest of the paragraph. It doesn't restate the main idea.

> Grade level:  below
> Lexile estimate:  730L

**Name(s):** _____

# Informative Paragraphs

## ➤ Part One

Discuss with your small group the characteristics of each informative paragraph. Take notes in the appropriate sections of the chart.

| | **"Energy from the Sun"** | **"Solar Power"** |
|---|---|---|
| The topic sentence clearly introduces what the paragraph will be about. | | |
| The paragraph has facts, definitions, details, and examples to explain the topic to readers. | | |
| Related ideas are grouped together. | | |
| The concluding sentence relates to the topic and the information in the paragraph. | | |

## ➤ Part Two

Answer the following questions with your group. Write your answers on a separate piece of paper.

1. What is each paragraph about? How do you know?

2. Which details help you understand the topic?

3. Which sentence restates the main idea?

4. How do the two paragraphs differ?

**Name(s):** _____

# Wave Energy

Ocean waves crash to the shore with powerful force. Scientists would like to find ways to harness this form of renewable energy. Wave energy comes from the wind that moves across the ocean's surface. Waves carry great amounts of energy. A device on the surface of the water can capture the energy when the waves move it up and down. Another method is to put tubes underwater. The waves move the tubes, and the tubes turn a turbine to generate power. If waves move into a large reservoir of water near the coastline, it is possible to force receding waves into a tube to turn a turbine. The energy from waves has great potential as a renewable power source.

Answer the first question, share your ideas with classmates, and then answer the second question.

1. What do you notice about this paragraph?

   _____
   _____
   _____
   _____

2. What did you learn from talking with classmates?

   _____
   _____
   _____
   _____

---

### Teacher Notes

Grade level:  appropriate
Lexile estimate:  870L

---

**Name(s):** _____

# Ocean Power

It is possible to get energy from the ocean. We see the ocean's power when large waves crash on the shore. Moving water can be used to turn turbines, which generate electricity. The technology to get power from waves is expensive. Waves can be forced into a narrow area so they are stronger. The ocean is a renewable source of energy, which makes it good for the environment. Not every place where people live is near an ocean, so this power source would not be available for everyone.

Answer the following questions. Then share your ideas with a classmate.

1. What do you notice about this paragraph?

   _____

   _____

2. How well does it match the characteristics of an informative paragraph?

   _____

   _____

3. What would you change? Rewrite the paragraph below. Then share your ideas with a partner.

   _____

   _____

   _____

   _____

   _____

   _____

   _____

   _____

   _____

   _____

┌────────────────────────────────────────┐
│           **Teacher Notes**              │
│ Grade level:  appropriate                │
│ Lexile estimate:  800L                   │
└────────────────────────────────────────┘

# Topic Sentences

## ➤ Objective

Students will read a sample paragraph, write possible topic sentences, work together to group information about a topic, and brainstorm to begin planning the writing of their own informative paragraphs.

## ➤ Introduction

*Our focus today is the topic sentence of an informative paragraph. You will practice writing topic sentences and grouping related information. This will help you begin to plan how to write your own informative paragraph.*

## ➤ Instruction

*The topic sentence clearly states the main idea of an informative paragraph. It gives readers an idea of the information they will read about. State the topic in an interesting way so readers will want to continue reading the paragraph.*

## ➤ Guided Practice

Think aloud to model writing a topic sentence. *First, consider what the paragraph will be about. That is the topic. Then think about the main idea you want to say about that topic.* Write on a whiteboard or chart paper. *For example, if your topic is wind power and your main idea is how it works, you could write, "Wind power uses moving air to generate electricity." What can I expect to read about in this paragraph?* (how wind power uses moving air to make electricity)

Distribute "Renewable Energy from Nature" (page 62). *Read the sample paragraph. Write possible topic sentences in Part One. Exchange papers with a classmate to complete Part Two.*

Distribute "Ideas that Go Together" (page 63). *Work with a group to complete this collaborative activity.*

## ➤ Independent Practice

*Which aspect of alternate energy sources most intrigues you? Think about a topic for the informative paragraph you will write.* Distribute "Plan Your Paragraph" (page 64). Review with students the possible topics listed in the activity. *What do you want to say about your topic? Combine your notes to write a topic sentence for your paragraph. Then complete Part Two.*

## ➤ Review

Review student-generated topic sentences from "Renewable Energy from Nature." Discuss which sentences make effective topic sentences and why.

## ➤ Closing

*Today you practiced writing topic sentences and grouping information related to a specific topic. You brainstormed ideas to write your own informative paragraphs.*

**Name(s):** _____

# Renewable Energy from Nature

Some sources of renewable energy come from nature. Biodiesel is a fuel that is manufactured from vegetable oils or animal fat. It burns cleaner than petroleum diesel. Biomass refers to plant materials that can be burned to produce energy. A common example is burning wood to cook food or heat a house. Some places burn scrap from paper mills and lumber mills to produce electricity. As organic matter decomposes, it releases methane gas. As the gas rises, some landfills capture the methane in pipes to burn and produce electricity. These processes utilize natural organic materials that can be grown again and again. Therefore, biogas is a valid renewable source of energy.

## ➤ Part One

Read the paragraph above. Then answer the questions below.

1.  What is the topic sentence of this paragraph?

    _____

    _____

2.  Rewrite the topic sentence for this paragraph in a few different ways.

    _____

    _____

    _____

    _____

## ➤ Part Two

Exchange papers with a classmate. Then complete the activity below.

1.  Add a checkmark next to each sentence that would entice you to continue reading the paragraph.

2.  Write the reason(s) why the sentence(s) you checked is/are effective.

    _____

    _____

3.  Discuss your responses with your partner.

+-----------------------------------+
| **Teacher Notes**                 |
|                                   |
| Grade level: appropriate          |
| Lexile estimate: 930L             |
+-----------------------------------+

**Name(s):** _____

# Ideas that Go Together

In a small group, complete the activity below.

1.  Brainstorm a specific topic for an informative paragraph about an alternate energy source.

2.  Write one or more questions about the topic and share your questions with the group.

    _____

    _____

    _____

3.  Use the group's questions to guide your research. Contribute facts, details, definitions, and examples to the discussion.

4.  Use the chart below to categorize information in ways that make sense.

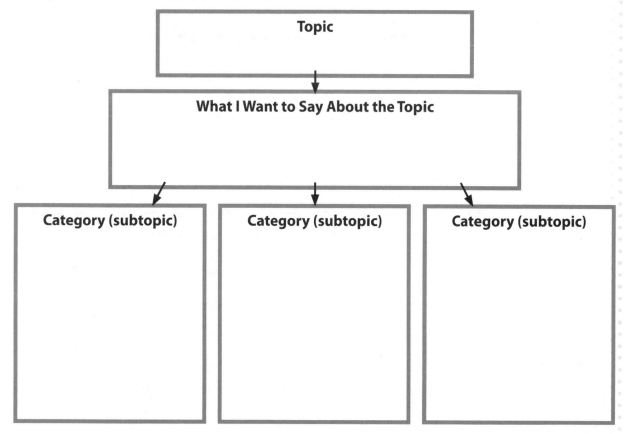

5.  Based on the information that the paragraph would address, write two or three possible topic sentences on your own. Then share your ideas with the group.

    _____

    _____

    _____

    _____

**Name(s):** _____

# Plan Your Paragraph

## ➤ Part One

Consider these topics related to alternate energy sources. You may have other ideas of your own.

- Renewable energy
- Concentrated solar power
- Wind turbines
- Hydroelectricity
- Geothermal energy
- Tidal power

Which aspect of alternate energy most intrigues you? Choose a specific topic for your informative paragraph.

| **My Topic** |
| --- |
| |

| **What I Want to Say About the Topic** |
| --- |
| |

Combine your notes from the boxes above to write a topic sentence for your paragraph.

_____

_____

_____

## ➤ Part Two

Based on what you want to say about your topic, ask questions to guide your planning and research.

List key words or phrases to begin to think about categories of information.

- _____
- _____
- _____
- _____

- _____
- _____
- _____
- _____

# Supporting Details

## ➤ Objective

Students will participate in a jigsaw activity to become familiar with different types of supporting details, consider details that could be added to an informative paragraph, and brainstorm topic-related details to include when they write their informative paragraphs.

## ➤ Introduction

*Today you will think about different types of supporting details for informative paragraphs and research to learn more about the topic you selected.*

## ➤ Instruction

*Supporting details help readers better understand the topic. This information may include facts, definitions, concrete details, quotations, or examples related to the topic. Group details together to emphasize each point you want to make about the topic. Use concrete nouns and vivid verbs to create a mental picture for your reader. Define any words specific to your topic that might be unfamiliar to readers.*

## ➤ Guided Practice

Distribute "Solar Power Words" (page 66). Divide students into groups and assign one category to each group. *Brainstorm details you could include in an informative paragraph about solar energy. For example, if your group is assigned facts, what is one fact you could include about solar power?* Conduct a jigsaw activity in which students from each group share their responses with students in other groups.

*Explanatory writing is a type of informative writing that tells how something works.* Distribute "Solar Energy" (page 67). *Work with a classmate to read the sample paragraph. Think about the types of details you could add to the paragraph to explain how solar power works.* Provide related research materials as available.

## ➤ Independent Practice

*Think about the topic you selected for your informative paragraph in the activity "Plan Your Paragraph" (page 64). Refer to your notes on "Plan Your Paragraph" to consider details that support your topic.* Distribute "Details About My Topic" (page 68). *Use this page to plan and research details you will include in your paragraph to support your topic sentence.*

## ➤ Review

Discuss student responses to "Solar Energy." Review possible details that could be added to the paragraph and suggest a logical order for the information.

## ➤ Closing

*You practiced thinking of details about a topic and adding details to an informative paragraph, and then brainstormed supporting details you will include in your informative paragraph.*

## ➤ Answers

"Solar Energy" (page 67); 1. solar power; 2. *suggested details*—descriptions of types of solar equipment (e.g., cells, panels, mirrors), how solar power is used to heat water or buildings, why there are different types of solar equipment (e.g., panels, mirrors), how people can use solar power in places that have cloudy days

Name(s): _____

# Solar Power Words

Think about how you could use your assigned category of details to write about solar power. Write ideas from your group in the appropriate category.

Then add details from other groups' responses as you share with classmates.

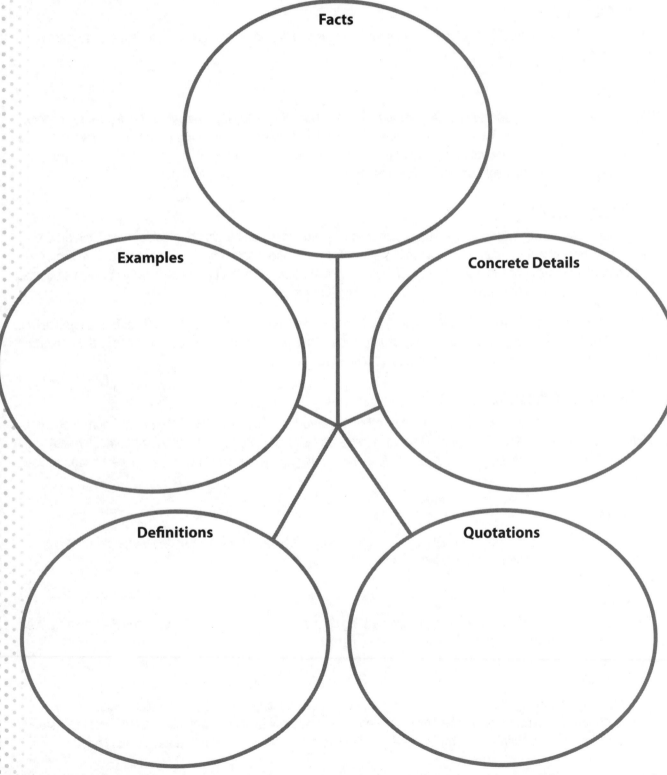

Name(s): _____

# Solar Energy

We get energy from the sun. With the right equipment, that energy can be converted to electricity. Solar power also heats water and buildings. Some solar equipment has panels, and other solar power plants have mirrors. People think solar power is only effective in places that receive a lot of sunshine. That's not entirely true. No matter where solar power is located, it takes a broad surface area to collect enough solar energy to be useful for large-scale power needs.

Work with a classmate to answer the questions below.

1. What is the specific topic of this paragraph?

   _____

2. What types of facts and details does this kind of paragraph need?

   _____

   _____

   _____

3. What details are missing from this explanatory paragraph?

   _____

   _____

   _____

4. What information would help support the topic?

   _____

   _____

   _____

   _____

## Teacher Notes

Grade level:  appropriate

Lexile estimate:  830L

**Name(s):** _____

# Details About My Topic

Write your topic sentence from "Plan Your Paragraph" (page 64).

_____

_____

Think about the types of supporting details that would fit best in your paragraph. Remember these tips:

- Consider what readers need to know.
- Include specific nouns and action verbs.
- Use a thesaurus and research materials.

Now complete the chart below.

| Facts | |
|---|---|
| Examples | |
| Concrete Details | |
| Definitions | |
| Quotations | |

On the back of this page, draw a diagram or picture that relates to your topic. Use your drawing to help you brainstorm more details to add to the chart above.

# Transition Words

## ➤ Objective

Students will identify transition words in sample paragraphs, practice adding such words to a sample paragraph, and practice using transition words in their own sentences about their chosen topics.

## ➤ Introduction

*Today we will think about how to connect sentences and ideas in our informative paragraphs so our writing makes sense for readers. To do this we use transition words, which are also called linking words.*

## ➤ Instruction

*Transition words connect sentences and ideas with main ideas to guide readers through an informative paragraph. Transition words have various purposes. Some show location or time. Others can compare or contrast concepts. Transition words can also emphasize a point or add information.*

## ➤ Guided Practice

Display sample paragraphs, such as "Solar Power" (page 57), "Wave Energy" (page 59), and "Renewable Energy from Nature" (page 62). *What transition or linking words do you notice in these paragraphs?* (if, other, another, as, therefore) *What purposes do these words have?* (to lead from one thought to another, to compare things or ideas, to show what happens next, to summarize or restate a reason) *What other transition words have you noticed in your reading?* Discuss additional examples of linking words and phrases, such as *for example*, *also*, and *because*. Display "Solar Energy" (page 67) and invite students to contribute their ideas to strengthen the paragraph. *What transition words can we add to connect ideas and make the writing flow more smoothly and make sense?* Think aloud to model using transition words and phrases to connect details with the main idea(s) of the paragraph.

## ➤ Independent Practice

*Distribute "Connecting Ideas" (page 70). Use your notes on "Details About My Topic" (page 68) to write sentences about your topic in Part One of "Connecting Ideas." Write appropriate transition words to connect ideas that go together in Part Two.* If time permits, prompt students to rewrite the sentences for their paragraphs in order.

## ➤ Review

*Check your work with a partner. Ask for and give feedback about connecting ideas and sentences together with transition words to help readers understand your writing.*

## ➤ Closing

*You identified transition words in informative paragraphs and thought about how to incorporate such words in a sample paragraph. You practiced using transition words in sentences about your topic for informative writing.*

Name(s): _____

# Connecting Ideas

## ➤ Part One

Use the supporting details listed on "Details About My Topic" (page 68) to write sentences about your informative topic.

_____

_____

_____

_____

_____

_____

_____

## ➤ Part Two

Rewrite your sentences from Part One to include transition words to connect ideas that go together. Use the word box below for ideas, or write other transition words and phrases that are appropriate for your sentences.

| also | for example | then |
|------|-------------|------|
| another | if | this is why |
| because | one way | so |

_____

_____

_____

_____

_____

_____

_____

_____

_____

# Concluding Sentences

## ➤ Objective

Students will discuss characteristics of effective concluding sentences, analyze samples, and practice writing concluding sentences for their informative paragraphs.

## ➤ Introduction

*An informative paragraph ends with a concluding sentence. You will discuss characteristics of concluding sentences with a partner and then practice writing concluding sentences for your informative paragraphs.*

## ➤ Instruction

*The concluding sentence of an informative paragraph relates to the information in the paragraph. It restates the topic sentence in different words or summarizes the main idea. A strong concluding sentence gives readers a sense that the paragraph is finished. If your paragraph explains parts of something or provides examples, the concluding sentence should tie it all together.*

## ➤ Guided Practice

Display or distribute copies of informative paragraphs from this module: "Wave Energy" (page 59), "Ocean Power" (page 60), "Renewable Energy from Nature" (page 62), and "Solar Energy" (page 67). Distribute "Concluding Sentences: Read and Write" (page 72) and pair students with a partner to read and analyze the concluding sentences from the paragraphs. *For Part One, evaluate the concluding sentences from paragraphs we have read in this module. With your partner, decide which concluding sentences answer which questions. For Part Two, write a concluding sentence based on what you wrote on "Plan Your Paragraph" (page 64). Share your response with your partner, and then revise it to restate your main idea more closely.*

If time permits, evaluate sample concluding sentences from available resources (e.g., materials students use for research). Have students share their findings.

## ➤ Independent Practice

*Write a statement about your topic. Then review your ideas and notes for your informative paragraph. Use your notes and feedback from a partner to rewrite your concluding sentence to more closely restate your main idea.*

## ➤ Review

*How did examining sample concluding sentences help you practice writing your own?* Discuss as a class.

## ➤ Closing

*Concluding sentences are important because they provide a definite end, or completion, to a paragraph. Leaving readers with a summary of the main idea helps them remember what they read.*

## ➤ Answers

"Concluding Sentences: Read and Write" (page 72): *suggested*—1. Wave Energy; 2. Ocean Power; 3. Solar Energy or Ocean Power; 4. Renewable Energy from Nature; 5. Wave Energy; 6. Wave Energy

Name(s): _____

# Concluding Sentences: Read and Write

## ➤ Part One

Work with a partner to review the teacher-selected paragraphs from this module and answer the questions below. The concluding sentences of these paragraphs may answer more than one question.

1.  Which paragraph has a concluding sentence that gives readers a better understanding of the topic?

    _____

2.  Which paragraph has a concluding sentence that confuses readers by adding new information?

    _____

3.  Which paragraph has a concluding sentence that includes detailed information that should be mentioned earlier in the paragraph?

    _____

4.  Which paragraph has a concluding sentence that summarizes the topic sentence?

    _____

5.  Which paragraph has a concluding sentence that makes readers think?

    _____

6.  Which paragraph has a concluding sentence that restates the main idea in an interesting way?

    _____

## ➤ Part Two

Using "Plan Your Paragraph" (page 64), complete the activity below.

1.  Use your topic sentence to write a statement about your topic. This will be a draft of your concluding sentence.

    _____

    _____

    _____

2.  Ask your partner to read and evaluate the sentence.

3.  Use the feedback you received from your partner to rewrite your concluding sentence so that it restates the main idea more closely and summarizes the information presented in your paragraph.

    _____

    _____

    _____

# First Draft and Peer Review

## ➤ Objective

Students will write first drafts of their informative paragraphs, observe how to complete sentence frames using a sample paragraph, and complete sentence frames about classmates' informative paragraphs as a peer review.

## ➤ Introduction

*Today you will compile your topic sentence, details about your topic, and your concluding sentence into a first draft of your informative paragraph. You will work with a partner to review each other's first drafts and offer feedback.*

## ➤ Instruction

*When you write the first draft, you write sentences about all your ideas. This is when you start to bring together your thoughts and notes about your topic. In the process, you may discover you need more information about something you want to say. In a first draft, crossing out text and making notes in the margins is acceptable and expected. First drafts are also called rough drafts: they are messy, and that's okay.*

## ➤ Guided Practice

Guide students through writing their first drafts. *Write your topic sentence from "Plan Your Paragraph" (page 64). Refer to your notes from "Details About My Topic" (page 68) to write one or more sentences for each idea in your informative paragraph. Copy your concluding sentence from "Concluding Sentences: Read and Write" (page 72).*

Distribute "A Different Perspective" (page 74). Read aloud the sample paragraph and model the activity by completing the sentence frames aloud.

## ➤ Independent Practice

Pair students with a partner to review students' first drafts of their informative paragraphs. *Read your partner's first draft and complete the sentence frames on page 74 to provide feedback. Focus on how your partner incorporated characteristics of informative writing in his or her paragraph. Then suggest ways he or she could make the paragraph more engaging for readers.*

## ➤ Review

Answer any questions as students write their first drafts. Review how to offer positive feedback and constructive criticism as needed.

## ➤ Closing

*You have written your first draft of your informative paragraph and received feedback on your writing from a classmate.*

## ➤ Answers

"A Different Perspective" (sample paragraph) (page 74):  1. renewable energy, it is stated in the topic sentence; 2. define renewable and nonrenewable energy sources, examples of renewable energy sources, uses of renewable energy; 3. such as, at some point, for years, another, other; 4. summarizing the need for renewable energy sources

**Name(s):** _____

# A Different Perspective

Renewable energy comes from sources that we can use over and over again. Some energy sources, such as fossil fuels and uranium, have limited quantities. At some point they will be used up. Renewable energy is not a new concept. For years, people have used wind and water power in various ways. Wind power and hydropower are just two examples of renewable energy. Another example is solar power. We use these renewable energy sources and others to produce electricity. Other uses of renewable energy include heating buildings and water, and providing fuel for transportation. The ongoing need for energy makes it important to continue to develop renewable energy sources.

Exchange first drafts and this page with a partner. Read your partner's paragraph and complete the sentences below to give feedback to your partner. Answer any questions your partner has about your comments to help him or her with ideas for improving his or her writing.

1. I can tell your paragraph is about _____

   because _____.

2. Highlight strong details (facts, definitions, examples) in the paragraph. These interesting details help me understand the topic:

   _____

   _____

   _____

3. This paragraph has these linking words and/or phrases, which connect ideas:

   _____

   _____

4. Your concluding sentence ended your paragraph by _____

   _____.

5. You could make your paragraph more engaging by doing this:

   _____

   _____

   _____

---

### Teacher Notes

Grade level: appropriate

Lexile estimate: 830L

---

# Second Draft and Self-Evaluation

## ➤ Objective

Students will discuss questions to guide them as they write their second drafts and then use a rubric to evaluate their writing.

## ➤ Introduction

*We will discuss questions to help you look closely at your writing as you write your second draft. You will then use a rubric to evaluate your second draft.*

## ➤ Instruction

*When we evaluate our writing, we look closely at it. We can ask questions and use a rubric to guide our revision process. This rubric is a learning tool. It shows the characteristics of effective informative writing. We can focus on a specific aspect and think about how we are doing in meeting these goals in our writing.*

## ➤ Guided Practice

*What is the purpose of informative writing?* (to examine a topic and convey ideas and information clearly) *We can ask the same types of questions a reporter would ask to make sure our paragraphs have all the necessary information.* Discuss the following questions with the class.

- *Why did you write this piece?* (to examine a topic and convey ideas and information about the topic)
- *Who will read your informative paragraph?* (answers may vary; readers who want to learn about the topic)
- *What will readers need to know?* (details that help them better understand the topic: facts, definitions, examples)
- *How will you tell them?* (group details in a way that clearly relates to the topic and main idea(s) about the topic; use linking words to guide readers through the information)
- *Where will they find important information in your paragraph?* (in specific details about the topic; the concluding sentence will summarize or restate the main idea)

Model how the questions might relate to the rubric. For example, *we learn from the rubric that important information in a paragraph should be grouped together in a logical way.*

## ➤ Independent Practice

*Think about the questions we discussed as you write a second draft of your informative paragraph.*

Distribute "Self-Evaluation: Informative Paragraph" (page 76). *Use the rubric to check how well your informative paragraph answers the questions from our class discussion.*

## ➤ Review

Answer any questions about the rubric and clarify as needed. Prompt students to share ways using the rubric can help them learn how to write informative paragraphs.

## ➤ Closing

*You answered questions about informative writing and used a rubric to evaluate and look closely at the second draft of your informative paragraph.*

# Self-Evaluation: Informative Paragraph

**Name:** _____     **Score:** _____

|  | **4** | **3** | **2** | **1** |
|---|---|---|---|---|
| **Topic Sentence** | My paragraph introduces a topic about alternate sources of energy in an interesting way. It has a clear topic sentence. | My paragraph has a clear topic sentence about alternate sources of energy. | The topic of alternate energy sources is mentioned in my paragraph. | It is unclear if my paragraph is about alternate energy sources. |
| **Organization** | Related information and ideas in my paragraph are organized in a logical way to emphasize specific points about my topic. | Related information and ideas are grouped together in a way that makes sense. | Some information and ideas are grouped together. | Information and ideas are not organized in a way that makes sense. |
| **Details** | My paragraph has facts, definitions, concrete details, and examples that clearly develop my topic about alternate energy sources. | My paragraph has facts, definitions, details, and examples about alternate energy sources. | My paragraph has some details, such as facts, definitions, or examples, about alternate energy sources. | My paragraph does not have many details about alternate energy sources. |
| **Transition Words** | I use a variety of transition words to connect my sentences and ideas back to the main idea of my paragraph. | I use transition words to connect ideas within my paragraph. | I use at least one transition word to connect ideas within my paragraph. | I do not use any transition words to connect ideas. |
| **Concluding Sentence** | My paragraph has a concluding sentence that summarizes the information and restates my main idea about alternate energy sources. | My paragraph has a concluding sentence that closely relates to my main idea about alternate energy sources. | My paragraph has a concluding sentence that is about alternate energy sources. | My paragraph does not have a clear concluding sentence, or the concluding sentence is not about alternate energy sources. |

On the back of this page, write two or three sentences describing what you learned about your writing and your revision process by thinking about the discussion questions and using this rubric.

# Final Draft

## ➤ Objective

Students will work in small groups to create visual aids for final proofreading and revision of student work and then write final drafts of their informative paragraphs.

## ➤ Introduction

*Today we will think about proofreading and final revisions that need to be made to a rough draft before writing a final draft. You will work with classmates to create a visual aid and then write the final draft of your informative paragraph.*

## ➤ Instruction

*A final draft is as correct as possible; words and sentences are capitalized correctly and have correct spelling, punctuation, and grammar. Sometimes informative or explanatory text has illustrations to help readers understand the content. The author has reviewed the information to make sure it is organized as logically as possible to develop the topic.*

## ➤ Guided Practice

Distribute "Writing Conventions" (page 78) and divide students into small groups. *Work with your group to draw a small picture for each aspect of writing conventions (spelling, capitalization, punctuation, grammar) that will remind others of things they will check and revise in their writing.* Provide scaffolding for students as needed.

## ➤ Independent Practice

*Refer to one of the visual aids your classmates created, either from your group or another group, to check your second draft for needed corrections. Then write a final draft of your informative paragraph.*

## ➤ Review

Review the conventions students will check in their proofreading (spelling, capitalization, punctuation, grammar). Discuss strategies students can use to recognize errors in their writing in these areas and how they might correct identified errors (e.g., conferences, digital tools such as spell check).

## ➤ Closing

*You created a visual reminder about how to proofread for correct use of conventions in your writing and then wrote a final draft of your informative paragraph.*

**Name(s):** _____

# Writing Conventions

With your small group, create a visual aid to help classmates when they revise their paragraphs to write a final draft. For each convention, draw and label a picture in the oval as a symbolic reminder. In the box next to it, describe how to proofread and revise your writing for this convention.

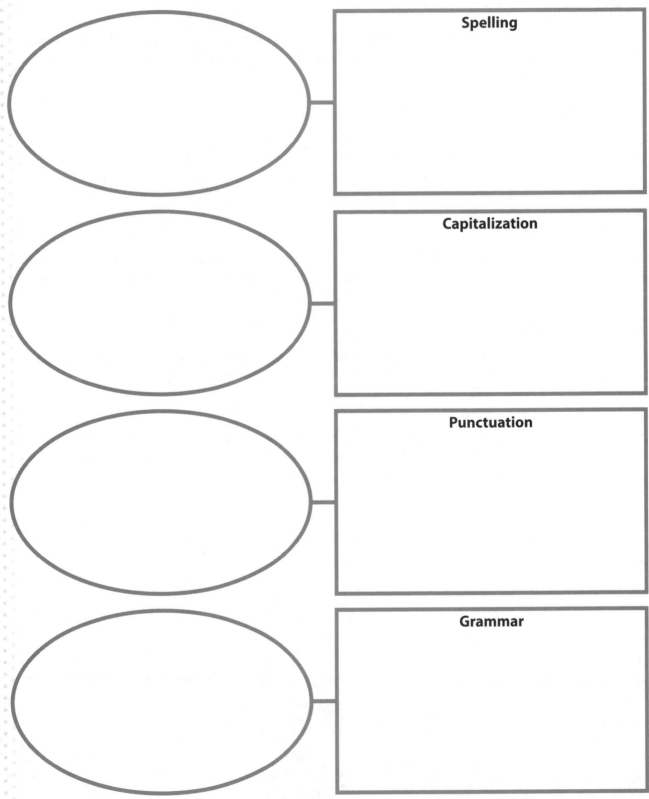

**Spelling**

**Capitalization**

**Punctuation**

**Grammar**

# Final Evaluation

## ➤ Objective

Students will compare the scores from their self-evaluations ("Self-Evaluation: Informative Paragraph" [page 76]) with their teacher evaluation scores, color diagrams, and reflect on their learning and improvement in writing.

## ➤ Introduction

*Today you will receive the scores I assigned to your informative paragraph and compare them with the self-evaluation you completed in a previous lesson.*

## ➤ Instruction

*In a previous lesson, you completed a self-evaluation activity in which you used a rubric to score your informative paragraph. We use rubrics as a learning tool to measure and analyze progress and improvement in specific areas. The informative paragraph rubric describes the characteristics of informative writing. How would you summarize or describe effective informative writing in one sentence?* (It examines a topic and conveys ideas and information clearly.)

## ➤ Guided Practice

Distribute "Powerful Writing" (page 80) and a variety of colored pencils, and return the final drafts with attached teacher evaluations (page 81). Using the activity page, model how to color different parts of the grid by talking through each aspect of an informative paragraph described on the rubric. *What score did you give yourself for the topic sentence? Color the square on the grid that corresponds to that score. Now check the score I gave you for your topic sentence. Use a different-colored pencil to mark the corresponding part of the grid for that score. Continue to compare scores and color corresponding parts of the grid for each characteristic described on the rubrics. Then complete Part Two.* Answer questions as needed while students work through the activity.

## ➤ Independent Practice

*Refer to the reflective sentences you wrote on "Self-Evaluation: Informative Paragraph." How did you apply your learning to writing your final draft? Write two or three sentences describing what you learned about your writing from reading and comparing the scores you received from me with the scores from your self-evaluation.*

## ➤ Review

Review the "Teacher Evaluation: Informative Paragraph" rubric for students' informative paragraphs, answering questions and clarifying as needed.

## ➤ Closing

*You received an evaluation of your informative paragraph from me, compared the scores with those from your self-evaluation, and reflected on your learning and writing improvement.*

Name(s): _____

# Powerful Writing

## ➤ Part One

1.  Refer to your scores on "Self-Evaluation: Informative Paragraph" (page 76). Use a colored pencil to shade each corresponding part of the grid below.

2.  Refer to the scores you received on "Teacher Evaluation: Informative Paragraph" (page 81) for your informative paragraph. Use a different-colored pencil to shade the equivalent parts of the grid for each part of your paragraph.

| Self-Evaluation Scores | | | | | Teacher Evaluation Scores | | | | |
|---|---|---|---|---|---|---|---|---|---|
| Topic Sentence | 4 | 3 | 2 | 1 | Topic Sentence | 4 | 3 | 2 | 1 |
| Organization | 4 | 3 | 2 | 1 | Organization | 4 | 3 | 2 | 1 |
| Details | 4 | 3 | 2 | 1 | Details | 4 | 3 | 2 | 1 |
| Transition Words | 4 | 3 | 2 | 1 | Transition Words | 4 | 3 | 2 | 1 |
| Concluding Sentence | 4 | 3 | 2 | 1 | Concluding Sentence | 4 | 3 | 2 | 1 |

## ➤ Part Two

1.  Based on the scores, which overall evaluation indicates your writing is more "powerful" or effective?

    _____

    _____

2.  Which areas of your paragraph show improvement over the course of the revision process as indicated by increased scores?

    _____

    _____

    _____

    _____

    _____

    _____

    _____

# Teacher Evaluation: Informative Paragraph

**Student Name:** _____          **Score:** _____

| | 4 | 3 | 2 | 1 |
|---|---|---|---|---|
| **Topic Sentence** | The paragraph introduces a topic about alternate sources of energy in an interesting way. It has a clear topic sentence. | The paragraph has a clear topic sentence about alternate sources of energy. | The topic of alternate energy sources is mentioned in the paragraph. | It is unclear if the paragraph is about alternate energy sources. |
| **Organization** | Related information and ideas in the paragraph are organized in a logical way to emphasize specific points about the topic. | Related information and ideas are grouped together in a way that makes sense. | Some information and ideas are grouped together. | Information and ideas are not organized in a way that makes sense. |
| **Details** | The paragraph has facts, definitions, concrete details, and examples that clearly develop a topic about alternate energy sources. | The paragraph has facts, definitions, details, and examples about alternate energy sources. | The paragraph has some details, such as facts, definitions, or examples, about alternate energy sources. | The paragraph does not have many details about alternate energy sources. |
| **Transition Words** | The author uses a variety of transition words to connect sentences and ideas back to the main idea of the paragraph. | The author uses transition words to connect ideas within the paragraph. | The author uses at least one transition word to connect ideas within the paragraph. | The author does not use any transition words to connect ideas. |
| **Concluding Sentence** | The paragraph has a concluding sentence that summarizes the information and restates a main idea about alternate energy sources. | The paragraph has a concluding sentence that closely relates to a main idea about alternate energy sources. | The paragraph has a concluding sentence that is about alternate energy sources. | The paragraph does not have a clear concluding sentence, or the concluding sentence is not about alternate energy sources. |

# Review

## ➤ Objective

Students will review the definitions of informative and explanatory writing and write their own definitions based on reading sample paragraphs.

## ➤ Introduction

*We will review the definitions of informative and explanatory writing, and you will write your own definitions and observe differences in these two similar types of writing.*

## ➤ Instruction

*We have been learning about informative and explanatory writing, and you have written an informative paragraph. At the beginning of this module you learned that explanatory writing explains how something works or tells readers how to do something. In this lesson, you will read two more sample paragraphs and identify the aspects of informative or explanatory writing demonstrated in each.*

## ➤ Guided Practice

Distribute "Geothermal Energy" (page 83) and read the sample paragraph together as a class. *Which type of writing is this: informative or explanatory? (informative) How do you know? Let's write a definition of this type of writing based on what we notice about this sample paragraph.* Guide students to generate a definition that includes examining a topic to convey ideas and information. *What specific details can we add to our definition to better explain this type of writing?* (topic sentence; facts, definitions, details, examples; concluding sentence)

## ➤ Independent Practice

Distribute "The Wonder of Hydropower" (page 84). *What are the similarities and differences between the two paragraphs you have read?*

## ➤ Review

Review students' definitions from the activities and discuss the similarities and differences between the two types of writing. (They are very similar.)

## ➤ Closing

*You read two examples of informative/explanatory writing and defined these types of writing by thinking about how they are similar. You identified characteristics of this type of writing by comparing two paragraphs.*

## ➤ Answers

"Geothermal Energy" (page 83): 1. This paragraph defines and tells readers about geothermal energy. It explains how people use geothermal energy, but it also has other information, so it might be considered mostly informative; 2. Definition might include: Informative writing conveys ideas and information clearly to help readers understand a topic. It includes facts, definitions, details, and examples and has a topic sentence and a concluding sentence.

"The Wonder of Hydropower" (page 84): 1. It is an explanatory piece of informative writing. It explains how hydropower works.

**Name(s):** _____

# Geothermal Energy

Geothermal energy relies on heat underground. In some places, hot magma is closer to the ground than others. People use Earth's warmth to heat water and generate electricity. Scientists do not expect the heat in the center of Earth to change. This makes geothermal energy a renewable source of energy. Pumping hot water from deep underground creates pressure. The hot water turns to steam, which turns turbines to generate electricity. A geothermal heat pump transfers water through pipes just below Earth's surface. Heat in the ground warms the water, which is then used to heat a building. People have a history of using hot mineral springs for bathing and cooking. Hot water from underground and hot magma under the earth provide people with geothermal energy.

Read the paragraph above with classmates. Then complete the activity below.

**1.** Is this an informative or an explanatory paragraph? How do you know?

_____

_____

_____

**2.** Define this type of writing based on what you notice about the sample paragraph.

_____

_____

_____

### Teacher Notes

Grade level:  appropriate
Lexile estimate:  850L

**Name(s):** _____

# The Wonder of Hydropower

Moving water has energy. It can be used to generate power. We call this energy source *hydropower* or *hydroelectric power*. It is a renewable energy source that relies on flowing water and a drop in elevation. We find these elements in nature. Rainfall replenishes the water in the river. A dam stops the flow of the river and creates a reservoir. The stored water builds up potential energy. When water is released, it rushes down through the dam and turns blades in a turbine. The turbine spins a generator, which produces electricity. Electricity is transmitted through power lines to homes and businesses. Engineers control the amount of water released through the dam based on electricity needs. Water can be stored in the reservoir for times when more power is needed. Hydropower is an effective renewable source of energy.

Read the paragraph above. Then answer the questions below.

**1.** What type of paragraph is this? How can you tell?

_____

_____

_____

**2.** How is this paragraph similar to "Geothermal Energy" (page 83)? How is it different?

_____

_____

_____

### Teacher Notes

Grade level: appropriate

Lexile estimate: 750L

# Introductory Paragraphs

## ➤ Objective

Students will brainstorm ideas about topics, identify their general points, and develop plans for researching the topics for writing informative/explanatory essays.

## ➤ Introduction

*You have worked with informative and explanatory paragraphs. Now we will focus on informative and explanatory essays. You will brainstorm a topic and group related ideas, then begin to plan your essay. Our topic for this module is polar change and exploration.*

## ➤ Instruction

*The introductory paragraph for an informative essay contains a thesis statement that introduces the topic. In informative or explanatory writing, the thesis statement gives the main idea of the essay. This first paragraph gives readers an overview of the information that will be discussed in the body of the essay. Brainstorming and drafting an introductory paragraph will help you identify which ideas you will need to research.*

## ➤ Guided Practice

*How can we identify the thesis statement in an introductory paragraph?* Discuss. Distribute "Polar Exploration" (page 86). *Read the sample paragraph and answer the questions.* Invite volunteers to share their responses. *When someone mentions the North Pole, South Pole, or phrases with the word "polar," what comes to mind?* Together as a class, discuss possible related topics for informative and/or explanatory essays. Conduct a whole-class brainstorming session using a whiteboard or chart paper to introduce potential prompts (see "Writing Topics" [pages 155–156]).

## ➤ Independent Practice

*Think about the possible topics we discussed together.* Distribute "Planning My Essay" (page 87). *Brainstorm a topic you would like to research and write about in an informative or explanatory essay. Then discuss your ideas with a partner and help each other group related ideas into categories for planning and research.* Define and explain research as needed. *Answer the planning questions at the bottom of the page.*

## ➤ Review

Review and discuss student responses to the planning questions in Part Two of "Planning My Essay" to guide students as they think about writing their informative essays.

## ➤ Closing

*Today you learned about thesis statements and introductory paragraphs in informative and explanatory essays. You brainstormed topics and grouped related ideas for further planning and research.*

## ➤ Answers

"Polar Exploration" (page 86): 1. *Thesis statement*—When it comes to exploration, no area of Earth escapes people's curiosity, including the North and South Poles. 2. *Point #1*—information about polar expeditions; *Point #2*—details about the challenges polar explorers face; *Point #3*—the reasons people explore polar regions

**Name(s):** _____

# Polar Exploration

When it comes to exploration, no area of Earth escapes people's curiosity, including the North and South Poles. There have been many expeditions to the polar regions. Polar exploration presents a challenge to explorers because of the distance and severe climate. Throughout history, people have explored the poles for a variety of reasons. Successful polar explorers have a plan and a purpose.

Read the sample paragraph above and answer the questions below.

**1.** What is the thesis statement?

_____

_____

**2.** What information would you expect to read about in the essay?

| Point #1 | Point #2 | Point #3 |
|---|---|---|
|  |  |  |

### Teacher Notes
Grade level: appropriate
Lexile estimate: 870L

# Planning My Essay

## ➤ Part One

Complete the graphic organizer by following the instructions below.

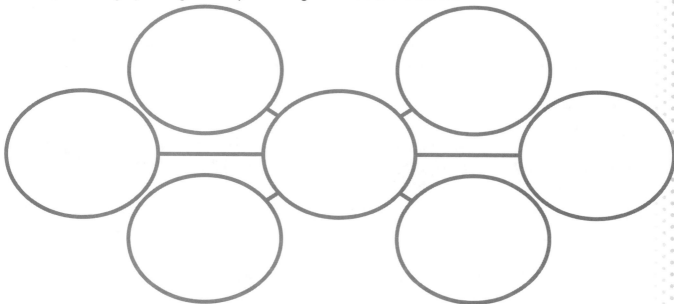

1. Write a key word about the topic of polar change or exploration in the center of the web.

2. Brainstorm everything you already know or want to learn about the topic. Write your words and ideas on different parts of the web.

3. Work with a partner to make connections between ideas. Draw arrows and other symbols to group your ideas and potential information into related categories.

## ➤ Part Two

After completing Part One, answer the questions below.

1. What do you want readers to learn from your essay? Why?

   _____

   _____

2. How will you convey the information in an interesting way?

   _____

   _____

3. Which ideas and subtopics from your web will you need to research?

   _____

   _____

4. On the back of this page, write two or three questions to guide your research.

# Body Paragraphs

## ➤ Objective

Students will learn about different ways to organize information in an informative essay and practice using two organizational structures. Then they will complete outlines for their chosen formats.

## ➤ Introduction

*Today you will learn about ways you can organize information and consider the best structure for your informative essay. You will also think about other formatting features to include in your essay.*

## ➤ Instruction

*Body paragraphs form the main part of your essay; they are the paragraphs after the introductory paragraph and before the concluding paragraph. The introductory paragraph introduces the main points, and there will be one paragraph for each main point of your essay. Each body paragraph is a complete paragraph, with a topic sentence, details about the main idea of the paragraph, and a concluding sentence.*

*We organize information in essays in a way that makes sense.*

## ➤ Guided Practice

*You can organize the information in your essay in one of several ways.* Distribute "Structure for My Essay" (page 89) and divide students into small groups. *Discuss with your small group each of the given ways to organize information, and give examples of how each structure might be used in an informative essay. With your group, you will practice organizing information in sequential order.*

*Depending on the topic of your essay, another format might work better.* Distribute "North & South" (page 90). *In this activity, you will work with a partner to practice using the compare-and-contrast structure. Then you will think about which format best fits with the topic and information for your informative essay.*

## ➤ Independent Practice

*Now you will incorporate your notes and research into an outline that will guide you later when you write your first draft.* Distribute "My Polar Trek" (page 91). *Use this activity to bring together what you have learned about organizing your information, as well as your notes and research about your topic.*

## ➤ Review

Clarify different formats for informative/explanatory essays and think aloud to demonstrate how to incorporate notes and research into a sample outline. Discuss text features such as headings and illustrations and how they can add to reader comprehension.

## ➤ Closing

*You learned about different organizational structures for informative essays and determined which format would best fit with the topic and information of your informative essay.*

Name(s): _____

# Structure for My Essay

## ➤ Part One

Work with a small group to discuss different organizational structures for informative/explanatory essays. In the chart below, describe and explain each type of structure and give examples of how it could be used for an informative essay.

| | |
|---|---|
| **Compare and Contrast** | |
| **Informative** | |
| **Sequential** | |
| **Cause and Effect** | |
| **Explanatory** | |

## ➤ Part Two

Research with your group to learn about how the North Pole or South Pole has changed over time. Use print and online resources to create a timeline to describe the polar changes. This will give you practice thinking about sequential structure.

Name(s): _____

# North & South

## ➤ Part One

Work with a partner to read the paragraph and complete the activities below.

The North Pole and South Pole both have extreme climates. Due to the tilt of Earth's axis, they do not receive direct sunlight, even in summer. These two regions are always cold, but the South Pole is colder. The South Pole, also called Antarctica, is land surrounded by ocean. The frozen ice never warms up. There are also mountains, and the higher the elevation, the colder it gets. The North Pole, or Arctic, is really an ocean surrounded by land. Even though the ocean water is cold, it is warmer than the land. The winters in both regions are very cold and dark, with fierce storms.

1. Complete the Venn diagram to compare and contrast qualities of each geographic location.

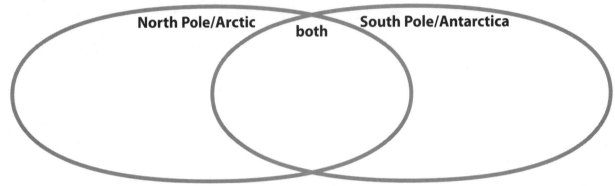

2. How might this information be written in an informative essay? Discuss your response with your partner.

_____

_____

## ➤ Part Two

1. Look back at the different organizational structures listed in Part One of "Structure for My Essay" (page 89).

2. Refer to your notes on "Planning My Essay" (page 87) to determine the best organizational structure for your essay.

3. Which structure best fits with your topic and the information that will be in your essay?

_____

_____

### Teacher Notes

Grade level: appropriate
Lexile estimate: 810L

# My Polar Trek

## ➤ Part One

On the back of this page, create an outline for your informative essay by following the instructions below.

1. Look at the descriptions and examples you wrote on "Structure for My Essay" (page 89) and think about the format that might best fit your essay.

2. Based on what you learned about your chosen essay structure in your small-group discussion, create an outline for the format you will use for your informative essay.

3. Incorporate your notes from "Planning My Essay" (page 87) and the information from your research to complete your outline.

## ➤ Part Two

Read about formatting features and then answer the questions below.

An author adds formatting features to an essay to help readers understand the organizational structure of the piece. One- or two-word **headings** give readers a brief overview of the sub-topics that the essay addresses. **Illustrations** can increase readers' understanding by showing a visual image of the concept the writing describes. **Captions** describe how a **photograph** or **drawing** relates to the text. **Charts**, **maps**, and **diagrams** are other types of images that help readers understand informative text.

1. What other formatting features would help readers understand your essay?

   _____

   _____

   _____

   _____

2. Name one feature that would enhance your essay and describe how it would add to your writing. If straight text would be best, explain why.

   _____

   _____

   _____

   _____

   _____

# Concluding Paragraphs

## ➤ Objective

Students will read classmates' essay outlines, provide feedback in the form of notes, and draft concluding sentences and concluding paragraphs.

## ➤ Introduction

*Today you will give and receive feedback on the essay outlines you wrote in a previous lesson. You will use the notes to draft a concluding paragraph that is interesting for readers.*

## ➤ Instruction

*The concluding paragraph in an informative essay summarizes the main points. A concluding sentence in the paragraph emphasizes the importance of the topic. The concluding paragraph in an explanatory essay will include the final step in the process. It may provide an overview of what has just been explained in the essay.*

## ➤ Guided Practice

*Exchange the outline you created on "My Polar Trek" (page 91) with a partner. Read your classmate's outline and provide feedback using "The End Is in Sight" (page 93). Use the notes you receive from your partner to think about how to summarize, review, and restate the main idea of your informative essay and draft a concluding paragraph.*

## ➤ Independent Practice

*Not only do we want to catch readers' interest at the beginning of an essay, but we also want to hold their attention all the way to the end. There is more than one interesting way to end an essay.* Read through the options for ending an essay on "A Captivating Conclusion" (page 94) with the class and explain each as necessary.

## ➤ Review

Review concluding sentences and paragraphs from sample print or online essays or short pieces and discuss techniques authors used to hold readers' interest to the end.

## ➤ Closing

*You used notes from a classmate to draft a concluding paragraph for your informative essay and practiced writing interesting concluding sentences.*

**Name(s):** _____

# The End Is in Sight

## ➤ Part One

Work with a partner and read each other's outlines created on "My Polar Trek" (page 91). Provide feedback to your partner by answering the prompts below.

**The topic or main idea of my classmate's essay is . . .**

**The main points in the essay are . . .**

## ➤ Part Two

Use the notes you receive from your partner to draft a concluding paragraph for your essay.

_____

_____

_____

_____

_____

_____

_____

_____

**Name(s):** _____

# A Captivating Conclusion

Continue to work with the draft of your concluding paragraph from "The End Is in Sight" (page 93). Practice writing a concluding sentence for your topic using each of the following techniques.

**Ask a question.**

**End with a quotation.**

**Describe the results (of what was explained), implications, or consequences (of information presented).**

**Offer a fresh perspective on what was said in the introduction.**

**Challenge readers with something to think about.**

# First Draft and Peer Review

## ➤ Objective

Students will write first drafts of their informative/explanatory essays and participate in a peer-review activity in which they read and mark classmates' essays then comment on them.

## ➤ Introduction

*Today you will compile your notes for an introductory paragraph, your outline, and the draft of your concluding paragraph to write a first draft of your informative essay. Then you will review and comment on a classmate's first draft.*

## ➤ Instruction

*When you write the first draft of your informative essay, incorporate all your notes from brainstorming and research. Start with the topic and main points you identified on "Planning My Essay" (page 87) and write an introductory paragraph. Be sure to include a thesis statement and introduce the main points you will discuss in your essay. Use your outline and notes from "My Polar Trek" (page 91) to write body paragraphs. Add the concluding paragraph draft you wrote on "The End Is in Sight" (page 93), incorporating the sentence from "A Captivating Conclusion" (page 94) you think fits best with your essay.*

## ➤ Guided Practice

Allow time for students to write first drafts of their essays.

Model how to mark text based on the guidelines provided on "A Reader's Perspective" (page 96). Distribute this page and green, orange, and blue colored pencils. Use an anonymous student essay or other sample to model the activity. *You will read a classmate's essay and use color to identify different aspects of the essay. Then you will complete a comment form to give your partner specific feedback.*

## ➤ Independent Practice

*Consider the comments you made about a classmate's essay and the comments you received from your partner. On your first draft, write notes about two things you plan to revise in your essay when you write your second draft.*

## ➤ Review

*What did you learn about writing an informative/explanatory essay from reading a classmate's essay and comments about your essay?* Review how looking at different aspects of an essay can ensure it includes the right amount of information to accomplish the author's purpose.

## ➤ Closing

*Today you wrote the first draft of your informative/explanatory essay and read a classmate's draft. You commented on your partner's draft and read comments about your essay.*

**Name(s):** _____

# A Reader's Perspective

## ➤ Part One

Read the first draft of your partner's informative/explanatory essay.

1. Use a green colored pencil to mark places where the author conveyed information or explained the topic well.

2. Use an orange colored pencil to draw an asterisk (*) next to places where additional information would help you better understand what the author is saying.

3. Use a blue colored pencil to draw arrows to show words or phrases that connect ideas.

4. Use a blue colored pencil to circle concrete words and details that help you understand the topic.

5. Use a blue colored pencil to underline the thesis statement.

6. Use a blue colored pencil to box the concluding sentence within the concluding paragraph.

## ➤ Part Two

Use the form below to give feedback to your partner about his or her essay. Then trade papers.

Your name: _____    Essay topic: _____

Essay author: _____    Essay type: ☐ Informative  ☐ Explanatory

How did you know the essay type? _____

_____

Based on the introductory paragraph, what did you expect the essay to be about?

_____

_____

How did the author incorporate specific details (e.g., facts, definitions, examples, or other information) to explain the topic?

_____

_____

What technique did the author use in the concluding paragraph?

_____

What could the author add to the essay to help readers better understand the topic?

_____

_____

# Second Draft and Self-Evaluation

## ➤ Objective

Students will write second drafts of their informative/explanatory essays and participate in a self-evaluation activity.

## ➤ Introduction

*Today you will write the second draft of your essay, use a rubric to evaluate your writing, and reflect on the strengths and weaknesses of your informative essay.*

## ➤ Instruction

*This rubric is similar to the one you used to evaluate your informative paragraph.* What have you learned since then about informative writing? Discuss with students. *As you use the rubric to evaluate your writing, think about the strengths and weaknesses you notice in your essay. In which areas did you give yourself higher or lower scores? When you think about changes you want to make in your second draft, you are making decisions about improving your writing.*

## ➤ Guided Practice

*Let's review the specific characteristics of an informative essay that I will look for when I read your essays.* Distribute "Self-Evaluation: Informative Essay" (page 98). *Read through the first draft of your essay. Note any revisions you want to make based on our discussion of the rubric.*

## ➤ Independent Practice

*Refer to the notes you received from your partner on "A Reader's Perspective" (page 96) and the revision notes you made in class today to write a second draft of your informative essay. After you have written your second draft, use the "Self-Evaluation: Informative Essay" to evaluate your writing.* Model how to make a T-chart for students to describe the strengths and weaknesses of their drafts. *Identify the areas in which you scored your draft higher or lower to determine strengths and weaknesses in your essay. Describe the strengths and weaknesses on the back of the self-evaluation page.*

## ➤ Review

Review the checklist with students and answer any questions about how they will score their second drafts.

## ➤ Closing

*Today you used a rubric to identify strengths and weaknesses in your second draft. Use your rubric scores and the T-chart you completed to write a final draft of your informative essay. Bring your final copy to class for the next lesson.*

# Self-Evaluation: Informative Essay

**Name:** _____     **Score:** _____

|  | 4 | 3 | 2 | 1 |
|---|---|---|---|---|
| **Introductory Paragraph** | My essay has an introductory paragraph that introduces a topic about polar change or exploration clearly and in an interesting way. It has a clear thesis statement. | My essay has an introductory paragraph with a clear thesis statement about polar change or exploration. | My essay has an introductory paragraph that mentions the topic of polar change or exploration. | The topic of my essay is unclear in the introductory paragraph. |
| **Organization** | Related information and ideas in my essay are organized in a logical way to emphasize specific points about polar change or exploration. | Related information and ideas about polar change or exploration are grouped together in paragraphs. | Some information and ideas about polar change or exploration are grouped together. | Information and ideas about polar change or exploration are not organized in a way that makes sense. |
| **Details** | My essay has facts, definitions, concrete details, and examples that clearly develop my topic of polar change or exploration. | My essay has facts, definitions, details, and examples about polar change or exploration. | My essay has some details, such as facts, definitions, or examples, about polar change or exploration. | My essay does not have many details about polar change or exploration. |
| **Transition Words** | I use a variety of transition words to connect ideas about the main point of each paragraph in my essay. | I use some transition words to connect ideas within each paragraph of my essay. | I use at least one transition word to connect ideas within my essay. | My essay does not have any transition words to connect ideas. |
| **Concluding Paragraph** | My essay has a concluding paragraph that summarizes the information and restates the main idea about polar change or exploration. | My essay has a concluding paragraph that closely relates to my main point about polar change or exploration. | My essay has a concluding paragraph that is about polar change or exploration. | My essay does not have a clear concluding paragraph, or the concluding paragraph is not about polar change or exploration. |

On the back of this page, create a T-chart to describe the strengths and weaknesses in your draft based on your evaluation of your essay.

# Review

## ➤ Objective

Students will read a sample essay and identify characteristics of informative/explanatory writing.

## ➤ Introduction

*You will review the characteristics of informative and explanatory writing and identify them in a sample essay. You will then analyze the essay further to complete a graphic organizer and answer questions.*

## ➤ Instruction

*What are the characteristics of informative and explanatory essays?* Discuss with the class. *The focused review you did of a classmate's draft and the rubric you completed to evaluate your own writing summarized key features of this type of writing. As you read sample essays today, consider how the author(s) communicate(s) ideas and information in a way that adds to readers' understanding of the topic.*

## ➤ Guided Practice

*You will work with classmates in groups of five to identify characteristics of explanatory writing in a sample essay.* Distribute "North Pole Changes" (page 100). Assign each student a number within their group of five students. *Read the sample essay together as a group. The person who is number one will read aloud the thesis statement. Other group members give a thumbs up/thumbs down signal to indicate whether or not this is indeed the sentence that states the topic or main idea for the essay. Each student will take a turn identifying a given writing feature as directed on the activity page.*

## ➤ Independent Practice

*Think about your small group's discussion of "North Pole Changes."* Distribute "A Closer Look" (page 101). *Refer to the sample essay to complete the graphic organizer and answer the questions at the bottom of the page.*

## ➤ Review

*How does analyzing sample informative and explanatory essays help you understand this type of writing? What did you learn from the activities in this lesson that you could apply to your own writing?*

## ➤ Closing

*You observed and discussed characteristics of a sample informative/explanatory essay. Think about what makes an informative essay effective as you continue to work on your final draft.*

## ➤ Answers

"North Pole Changes" (page 100): *thesis statement*—Scientists have observed that the magnetic North Pole, which is in the middle of the Arctic Ocean, shifts; *example*—Imagine that Earth is like a spinning top with the North Pole at the top and the South Pole at the bottom; *definition*—A glacier is a large amount of ice; *details*—Polar ice melts and refreezes with the change in seasons; *concrete words*—axis, experts, fascinating, massive, prior, track, wobble; *transition words*—a different, as, but, for, however, now, when; *concluding statement*—Each year, scientists track and record the magnetic location of the North Pole.

Name(s): _____

# North Pole Changes

Earth spins on its axis with the North Pole at the top and the South Pole at the bottom. Scientists have observed that the magnetic North Pole, which is in the middle of the Arctic Ocean, shifts. Scientists have different theories as to what causes this, but they agree it's related to climate change.

When you spin a top very fast, the tip on the top stays in a tight, small circle. The slower the top goes, however, the wider the circle of the tip. Now picture a top that is spinning at a medium speed. It may wobble a little. Earth is a top spinning at medium speed; the North Pole is wobbling a little. The good news is that it has always wobbled a little. Some experts in the field of climate change say that the North Pole is wobbling in a different direction. As years pass, the North Pole constantly moves. For the last several years, it has drifted south towards Canada. But now the North Pole is moving east, and at a much faster rate.

Why is this? Most scientists believe it is because of climate changes. A glacier is a massive block of ice. The more ice there is in the Arctic Ocean, the less it will melt in the summer. Recent summers have been warmer than average, causing more ice than normal to melt, leaving less ice to refreeze in the winter.

As more glaciers melt near the North Pole, the weight of all that water and ice move around. The more the weight moves around, the more the North Pole changes direction. One theory is that the ice is melting because humans are polluting Earth, which causes the air temperature to heat up.

A different perspective is that climate change happens in cycles. People with this perspective point to previous cycles in history, such as prior ice ages and times of warmer weather. Earth may be heating up now, but it will cool down later, as part of a normal climate cycle.

Each year, scientists track and record the magnetic location of the North Pole. Explorers will always be able to find their way to this fascinating area of our planet.

---

Work through the essay as directed below. As each group member identifies a specific part of the essay, give a thumbs up/thumbs down signal to indicate your opinion.

- **Student #1:** Identify and read aloud the thesis statement.

- **Student #2:** Identify one or more facts, definitions, or examples and explain how they relate to the main idea of the essay.

- **Student #3:** Identify one or more facts, definitions, or examples and explain how they relate to the main idea of the essay.

### Teacher Notes

Grade level: appropriate
Lexile estimate: 860L

- **Student #4:** Point out concrete words that add to the meaning of the essay and transition words that connect ideas.

- **Student #5:** Read aloud the concluding sentence and/or describe how the concluding paragraph restates the main idea and summarizes the main points of the essay.

**Name(s):** _____

# A Closer Look

Analyze the sample essay "North Pole Changes" (page 100) to complete the graphic organizer below. Draw arrows and write transition words and phrases to show relationships between ideas.

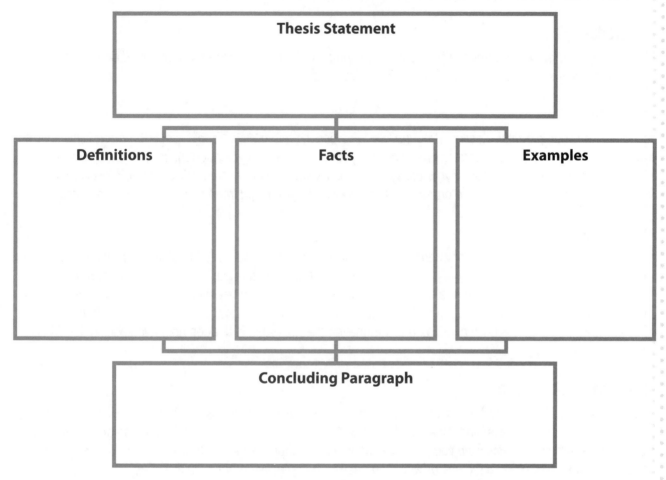

1. Based on the introductory paragraph, what ideas did you expect the author to discuss in the body paragraphs of the essay?

   _____

   _____

2. Write one cause-and-effect statement based on the information in the essay.

   _____

   _____

3. How did the author restate the thesis statement in the concluding paragraph? Write a sentence to summarize the topic and main points of the essay.

   _____

   _____

   _____

# Final Evaluation

## ➤ Objective

Students will compare the scores they received on their informative essays with their self-evaluations and consider the strengths and weaknesses of their writing.

## ➤ Introduction

*Today you will review your self-evaluation scores and compare them to the scores you received from me to think about the strengths and weaknesses of your informative essay.*

## ➤ Instruction

*You evaluated your informative essay using the "Self-Evaluation:  Informative Essay" (page 98) rubric. This showed you the characteristics I would look for when I scored your essays. When you used the rubric, you also reflected on the strengths and weaknesses of your essay. When you compare your scores with those you received from me, you will also complete reflective prompts to think about how you might improve your informative writing.*

## ➤ Guided Practice

*Which strengths and weaknesses of writing can be identified from understanding the characteristics of informative writing? Discuss with the class and create a T-chart on a whiteboard or chart paper. Which words or phrases on the rubric describe strengths of informative writing?* (introduce topic in an interesting way, include concrete details, use transition words or phrases to connect ideas, etc.) *Which descriptions on the rubric identify weaknesses in informative writing?* (topic is unclear, ideas and information are not organized, does not have specific details or transition words, etc.)

## ➤ Independent Practice

Distribute students' "Self-Evaluation:  Informative Essay" rubrics, "Teacher Evaluation:  Informative Essay" (page 103) rubrics, scored student essays, and "Changes for the Better" (page 104). *In the chart in Part One of "Changes for the Better," record your scores from your self-evaluation and teacher evaluation. In which areas do the scores most closely match? Compare the scores and then answer the reflective prompts in Part Two.*

## ➤ Review

Answer any questions students have about teacher evaluation scores. Discuss how the points on a rubric can help students identify strengths and weaknesses in their writing.

## ➤ Closing

*Discussing the characteristics of informative writing as described on a rubric and then comparing your self-evaluation with scores you received from another reader gave you the opportunity to consider strengths and weaknesses in your informative writing.*

# Teacher Evaluation: Informative Essay

Student Name: _____     Score: _____

|  | 4 | 3 | 2 | 1 |
|---|---|---|---|---|
| **Introductory Paragraph** | The essay has an introductory paragraph that introduces a topic about polar change or exploration in an interesting way. It has a clear thesis statement. | The essay has an introductory paragraph with a clear thesis statement about polar change or exploration. | The essay has an introductory paragraph that mentions the topic of polar change or exploration. | The topic of the essay is unclear in the introductory paragraph. |
| **Organization** | Related information and ideas in the essay are organized in a logical way to emphasize specific points about polar change or exploration. | Related information and ideas about polar change or exploration are grouped together in paragraphs. | Some information and ideas about polar change or exploration are grouped together. | Information and ideas about polar change or exploration are not organized in a way that makes sense. |
| **Details** | The essay has facts, definitions, concrete details, and examples that clearly develop the author's topic about polar change or exploration. | The essay has facts, definitions, details, and examples about polar change or exploration. | The essay has some details, such as facts, definitions, or examples, about polar change or exploration. | The essay does not have many details about polar change or exploration. |
| **Transition Words** | The author uses a variety of transition words to connect ideas about the main point of each paragraph in the essay. | The author uses some transition words to connect ideas within each paragraph of the essay. | The author uses at least one transition word to connect ideas within the essay. | The essay does not have any transition words to connect ideas. |
| **Concluding Paragraph** | The essay has a concluding paragraph that summarizes the information and restates the main idea about polar change or exploration. | The essay has a concluding paragraph that closely relates to the author's main point about polar change or exploration. | The essay has a concluding paragraph that is about polar change or exploration. | The essay does not have a clear concluding paragraph, or the concluding paragraph is not about polar change or exploration. |

Name(s): _____

# Changes for the Better

## ➤ Part One

Complete the chart using your "Self-Evaluation:  Informative Essay" (page 98) and "Teacher Evaluation: Informative Essay" (page 103) rubrics.

1.  Write the scores from your self-evaluation and your teacher evaluation in the chart below.

|  | Introductory Paragraph | Organization | Details | Transition Words | Concluding Paragraph |
|---|---|---|---|---|---|
| **Self Score** | | | | | |
| **Teacher Score** | | | | | |

2.  In which areas do the scores most closely match?

_____

_____

_____

_____

## ➤ Part Two

Complete the prompts below to reflect on your informative essay.

1.  I agree with the score I received for _____ because

_____

_____

_____ .

2.  I disagree with the score I received for _____ because

_____

_____

_____ .

3.  I don't understand the score I received for _____ , and I think

_____

_____

_____ .

# All About Narrative Writing

## ➤ Objective

Students will read examples of narrative writing that have strengths and weaknesses, and generate a working definition of this type of writing.

## ➤ Introduction

*Today we will explore narrative writing by reading examples and developing a working definition of this type of writing. During this module, your narratives will be about an experience with drones.*

## ➤ Instruction

*Narrative writing describes a real or imagined experience by using descriptive details to relate a sequence of events. The events happen to one or more individuals, also known as characters. Narratives often describe a personal experience that happened to the narrator. Readers may learn a lesson or gain insight from reading the account.*

## ➤ Guided Practice

Display and read "Birthday Drone" (page 107) together as a class, covering up the Teacher Notes. *What do you notice about this narrative paragraph? Let's create a list of characteristics of narrative writing.* Display and distribute "Characteristics of a Narrative Paragraph" (page 106). Work together as a class to complete the sentences. *Which of these characteristics do you observe in "Birthday Drone"? We'll check the box for each characteristic this narrative has.* Read "Flight of the Drones" (page 108). *Which characteristics of narrative writing do you notice in this example? Which sample paragraph is a stronger example of narrative writing? Why?*

## ➤ Independent Practice

Distribute "Race Day at the Park" (page 109) and "Flying Down the Aisle" (page 110). *Read each paragraph and complete the chart on page 106, checking boxes to indicate which narrative characteristics you notice in each example. Work with a partner to take turns explaining why you completed the chart as you did. Be prepared to state why you did or did not check a characteristic for each example.*

## ➤ Review

Review students' responses on the chart for the second set of examples.

## ➤ Closing

*Based on your observations of the narrative examples, how would you describe a narrative paragraph in one sentence?* (A narrative paragraph develops a real or imagined experience or event using descriptive words and sensory details.)

## ➤ Answers

"Characteristics of a Narrative Paragraph" (page 106):
Narrative writing develops a <u>real</u> or imagined experience or <u>event</u>.
The topic sentence establishes a <u>situation</u> and introduces a narrator and/or other <u>characters</u>.
The author uses <u>descriptive</u> words to enhance the <u>narrative</u>.
The author uses <u>sensory</u> details to convey an <u>experience</u> or event.
<u>Transition</u> words and phrases are used to guide readers through the related <u>actions</u> within an event.
The narrative has a <u>concluding</u> sentence that flows naturally from the narrated experience or event.

**Name(s):** _____

# Characteristics of a Narrative Paragraph

Work together with classmates to complete the sentences in the chart and identify characteristics of the first narrative sample (page 107). Check the boxes that apply to the sample. Then complete the activity by following the instructions below.

| Narrative Characteristics | Birthday Drone | Flight of the Drones | Race Day at the Park | Flying Down the Aisle |
|---|---|---|---|---|
| Narrative writing develops a _____ or imagined experience or _____. | | | | |
| The topic sentence establishes a _____ and introduces a narrator and/or other _____. | | | | |
| The author uses _____ words to enhance the _____. | | | | |
| The author uses _____ details to convey an _____ or event. | | | | |
| _____ words and phrases are used to guide readers through the related _____ within an event. | | | | |
| The narrative has a _____ sentence that flows naturally from the narrated experience or event. | | | | |

1. Read through the second narrative example (page 108). Check the boxes for each characteristic the narrative demonstrates.
2. Continue with the remaining narrative examples (pages 109 and 110).
3. Explain to a partner your reasoning for each trait you checked, as well as for boxes you did not check.

# Birthday Drone

I grasped Mom's hand in an effort to lure her to the toy store in the brightly lit mall and asked her if Dad would like a drone for his birthday. She sighed and followed me reluctantly, reminding me of the many gadgets he already had. Once in the store, I studied the display of drones. At first glance, they seemed like fancy helicopters. Reading had informed me they were more than they appeared. I explained to Mom how Dad could sit in his recliner and maneuver it to her. Then she wouldn't have to fetch stuff for him. I moved closer to the shelf to inspect the different models. Mom pointed out that Dad would still have to figure out how to attach things to the drone. She showed me a medium box that wasn't too expensive. I studied the box and noticed this model didn't have a camera, which I was sure he'd want. However, it would be way out of our price range to get a drone with a camera, and I wasn't sure I wanted Dad taking pictures of my brother and me all the time. I drifted back over to the display and picked up the basic model Mom had suggested. Mom took the drone to the register, and I followed, pleased with our selection.

---

## Teacher Notes

This example describes a real experience and has the following strengths and weaknesses:

- The topic sentence introduces the narrator (I), other characters (Mom and Dad), and the situation (buying a present for Dad's birthday).
- The narrative includes these descriptive words:  *gadgets, recliner, maneuver, inspection.*
- The narrative doesn't include many sensory details.
- The narrative includes these transition words and phrases:  *once, at first glance, then, however.*
- The concluding sentence flows naturally from the experience described in the story.

> Grade level:  appropriate
> Lexile estimate:  900L

# Flight of the Drones

Captivated, Colin inspected the store window display. The elaborate exhibit showcased a drone with every feature imaginable, as well as basic drones at entry-level prices. As far as Colin was concerned, drones represented the next best thing to flying. His mom was a pilot for a major airline, but he didn't get to fly nearly as often as he'd like. Colin scanned the placard next to the display. He checked the time and determined he had a few more minutes to browse before heading home to do chores and homework. Not everyone shared his fascination with drones. Three classmates—Jack, Madeline, and Sophia—laughed and ignored Colin as they passed the small hobby shop. When they had gone, Colin looked back at the drones. The signs claimed the new models had multiple rotors and propellers to add stability, even in heavy winds. The advertising lured Colin to take a tentative step toward the shop entrance. Colin glanced at his phone, then up into a friendly face. The storekeeper swept a mop of disheveled red hair behind his shoulders. He told Colin they were about to have a drone race in the back. Colin grinned, wondering how this guy knew he lived for racing. As he pocketed his phone, Colin followed him through the aisles to the rear of the store. Madeline stood to one side, cheering as the drones readied for takeoff in a small racing arena.

---

## Teacher Notes

This example has the following strengths and weaknesses:

- The topic sentence introduces the main character (Colin) and mentions the setting (toy store window) but not the situation.
- The narrative includes these descriptive words: *exhibit, pilot, placard, rotors, propellers, stability, advertising.*
- The narrative doesn't include senses other than sight.
- The narrative includes these transition words and phrases: *as, when they had gone, then.*
- The concluding sentence affects the main character's emotions by adding an element of surprise.

> Grade level: appropriate
> Lexile estimate: 940L

Photograph ©Ted Eytan (*https://www.flickr.com/photos/taedc/15730191218/*), CC BY-SA 2.0.

# Race Day at the Park

My sister and I walked through the park last Saturday. Clouds parted occasionally, allowing the sun to shine through enough to brighten the shadows, but not enough to warm the air very much. As we came to the grassy area after the nature trail, we heard buzzing that sounded like a small helicopter. A half-dozen people were gathered, flying drones in the field. The first thing I noticed was the helmets they wore. A man in a black T-shirt and scruffy jeans introduced himself and explained they were a drone-racing hobby group. He showed us his helmet, and I was amazed when he let me try it on. The visor showed me a live feed from a drone flying around. It reminded me of a video game with a battery light

in the top right corner and a screen that showed the speed and other information. The drones flew around a track marked with colored ribbons on the trees. The drones had to fly in and out of the trees like it was an obstacle course. A guide told us that the whole track was about 100 × 100 feet, and one lap around was about an eighth of a mile. He pointed to a couple of tall stakes in the ground with a banner stretched between them. They would launch the drones near the banner. The drones would start on the ground and go up in the air, then maneuver through the track. My sister said that the drones didn't look like the ones we had seen in the stores. Our new friend explained that they customized their machines. The racers purchased individual components: propellers, weights, and circuit boards, and put them on homemade platforms. He showed us his drone, and we noticed these weren't basic, inexpensive components. They were built for racing. Everything except the circuit board could be replaced, which was good because he said they crashed a lot. We enjoyed spending time with this friendly group, watching them race their drones as a hobby.

---

## Teacher Notes

This narrative describes a real experience and has the following strengths and weaknesses:

- The topic sentence introduces the narrator (I), another character (sister), and the setting (the park) but not the situation.
- The author uses descriptive details to help readers imagine the actions within the event.
- The narrative includes these transition words and phrases: *as, the first thing.*
- The concluding sentence flows naturally from the described experience.

> Grade level:  appropriate
> Lexile estimate:  920L

# Flying Down the Aisle

Dad came to my twin brother and me and said he wanted to have an RC car take the rings down the aisle for his upcoming wedding. I gave this only a second's thought before I asked him what he thought about having a quadcopter take the rings instead. Dad loved the idea! He told me to research prices and models under $100 and let him know what I found. For once, Dad gave me plenty of time to gather the information he wanted. This would be tricky; the quadcopter had to be big enough to carry the rings without

affecting speed. I was happy to report that I had found one for only $50. The price was right, but I cautioned Dad that two rings might be too heavy for one quadcopter. Dad suggested we buy two and have one for each ring. My brother and I accompanied Dad to the store and showed him the correct model. Fortunately, the store had two in stock. Now we had three weeks before the wedding to learn to fly them. On my first test run it crashed into the ceiling and the walls, but it didn't get wrecked, and I could keep flying it. We tested it with the ring in a box, but that made it too heavy so we tied the ring to the quadcopter. Each one had a flight time of only ten minutes, so we couldn't do any fancy tricks, just a straight flight down the aisle. During dress rehearsal, we had two people on stage flying them in reverse. They launched them off the sound booth in the back. The day of the wedding, we piloted them from on stage. Once the pastor cued us to send the rings down, we launched them. From the top balcony they buzzed down like wasps, setting the guests astir. The audience gaped at these mechanical monsters delivering rings. With a couple of false landings, they made it to Dad's and Annika's outstretched hands. The motors wound to a stop, the audience's whispers quieted, and the ceremony resumed.

---

## Teacher Notes

This narrative describes a real experience and has the following strengths and weaknesses:

- The topic sentence introduces the narrator (me), other characters (Dad and twin brother), and situation (how to transport rings in a wedding).
- The narrative could use more descriptive words and sensory details.
- The narrative includes these transition words and phrases: *for once, now, on my first, so, during, the day of, once, with.*
- The concluding sentence makes sense as the final action in the event.

> Grade level: appropriate
> Lexile estimate: 860L

# Beginning the Narrative

## ➤ Objective

Students will begin to think about and plan their narrative paragraphs about drones. They will participate in activities in which they orient readers to their story contexts, introduce the narrators and/or characters, and organize actions within events.

## ➤ Introduction

*Today you will build upon what you have learned about narrative writing to think about and plan a narrative paragraph. You will ask and answer questions with a partner and plan how to orient readers to, or help readers understand the situation surrounding, your narrative story.*

## ➤ Instruction

*Within the first sentence of a short narrative piece, authors orient their readers. This means they introduce one or more main characters in a setting, and introduce the situation, or main event, through the point of view of the person telling the story. Before writing the entire narrative, you will want to plan and organize the sequence of actions within the main event in your story. As you consider the narrative you will write, think about times you have told someone about something that happened to you. Narratives include details in an order that makes sense. The details help readers understand the author's purpose in telling the story.*

## ➤ Guided Practice

*In narrative writing, experiences may be real or imagined. In your narrative, who is experiencing the actions that are part of the event? Who is telling the story? How do you know?* Distribute "Let Me Introduce You" (page 112). *Work with a partner to write and answer questions about experiences with drones to help you plan your narrative. Use this page to guide you as you write questions to ask your partner. Use the feedback you receive from your partner to help you plan and brainstorm ideas for your narrative.*

## ➤ Independent Practice

Distribute "Orient Your Reader" (page 113). *Use this page to plan how you will orient your readers to specific aspects of your narrative. Complete the graphic organizer with details about your narrator, setting, event/situation, and context. Then plan the actions that are part of the event described in your narrative on the page I'm passing out now.* Distribute "My Narrative Event Chart" (page 114).

## ➤ Review

Review characteristics of narrative writing as discussed in the previous lesson in the context of the questions students wrote and answered with their partners to check for understanding.

## ➤ Closing

*You asked and answered questions with a partner to brainstorm ideas for your narrative about drones. Then you planned the aspects of your writing that orient readers to the story situation: narrator, setting, main event, and context.*

**Name(s):** _____

# Let Me Introduce You

Write questions to ask your partner about each of the following aspects of your narrative. Record your partner's answers on the lines below the questions. Use the feedback you receive from your partner to help you plan and brainstorm ideas for your narrative.

**Narrator:** _____

**Actions**

_____

_____

_____

_____

_____

**Time and Setting**

_____

_____

_____

_____

_____

**Main Character's Goal**

_____

_____

_____

_____

_____

**Obstacle**

_____

_____

_____

_____

**Name(s):** _____

# Orient Your Reader

A drone is an unmanned vehicle that flies (UAV). Think about an experience you have had, or would like to have, or an experience someone else has had with drones. This might include any experience with a remote helicopter or plane, a situation in which such a vehicle might be used, or a time when you were observed by a drone.

Think about the things your reader needs to know about your story. Describe each aspect of your story in the graphic organizer below.

**Narrator**

Who is telling the story?

_____

_____

**Setting**

Where does the event take place?

_____

What does the narrator see, hear, smell, or touch in this place?

_____

_____

_____

_____

**Event/Situation**

What is the main thing that happens in this experience?

_____

_____

What is the problem in the story?

_____

_____

_____

**Context**

Why did the narrator experience the event?

_____

_____

_____

_____

**Name(s):** _____

# My Narrative Event Chart

A narrative describes a real or imagined experience in a natural sequence of actions that are part of the event. An event happens over a period of time—whether it be minutes or hours. Use the flowchart below to plan the actions that happen in your narrative.

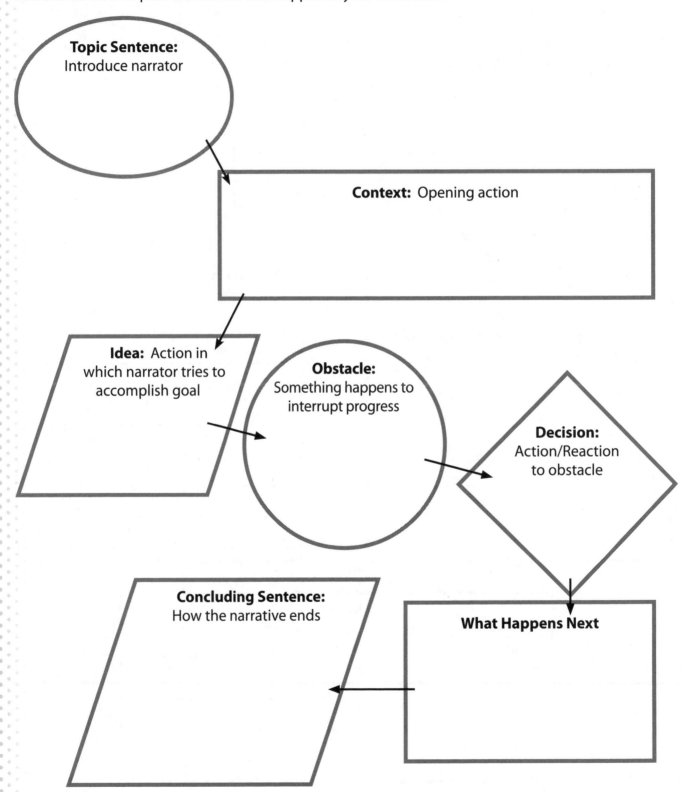

# Descriptive Words and Actions

## ➤ Objective

Students will brainstorm concrete and sensory detail words to use when writing their narratives. They will also practice using descriptive words to describe story events and experiences and create drawings to think about the action in their narratives.

## ➤ Introduction

*Today you will work with a partner to think about sensory details and find concrete words to describe people, places, and things in your narratives. You will also create drawings to show the characters' actions in your story.*

## ➤ Instruction

*Authors use concrete words and sensory details to describe events and experiences in a narrative. They describe how characters respond to situations in the story. Descriptive details provide readers with mental pictures about what happens in the narrative. Concrete words help readers understand actions within a story event.*

## ➤ Guided Practice

Distribute "Descriptive Details" (page 116). *Look at the photograph on the page. Work with a partner to complete Parts One and Two. Use concrete words and sensory details to describe objects and a setting that might be part of your story situation. Use a thesaurus to brainstorm concrete word choices to convey what you want to say.*

## ➤ Independent Practice

Distribute "Narrative Action" (page 117). *Refer to your notes from "Orient Your Reader" (page 113) to complete this page. Draw simple figures to represent the main person(s) in the narrative. Create several frames to show the actions in the story.*

## ➤ Review

Allow students to share and receive feedback on drawings. Clarify and answer any questions about using sensory words to write descriptions in a narrative.

## ➤ Closing

*You worked with a partner and used a thesaurus to explore concrete words that describe details in a narrative, and you drew pictures to show the character's actions.*

Name(s): _____

# Descriptive Details

## ➤ Part One

Work with a partner to brainstorm and write concrete words to describe the photograph below. Include words that describe sensory details: what you would see, hear, smell, or touch if you were in the setting of the photograph.

_____

_____

_____

_____

_____

_____

_____

_____

_____

_____

## ➤ Part Two

Follow the instructions below to complete the graphic organizer.

1. Think about the setting of your narrative and the events that happen as part of the experience. In the box on the left side of the graphic organizer, write the experience your narrative will describe.

2. On the center line, write several key words or concepts from your narrative, one word in each section.

3. On the lines above and below the center line, write concrete words and sensory details related to the key word. Use a thesaurus and input from a partner to help you.

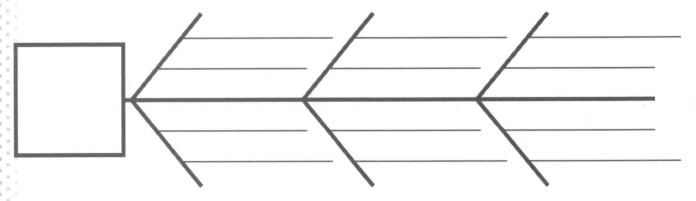

# Narrative Action

Refer to your notes from "Orient Your Reader" (page 113) to complete the activity below.

Who is telling the story? _____

Who else besides the narrator takes part in the experience?

_____

_____

How does the narrator interact with the other character(s)?

_____

_____

_____

_____

Draw simple figures in the boxes below to represent the main person(s) in the narrative. Create several frames to show the actions in the story.

| | | |
|---|---|---|
| | | |

# Transition Words

## ➤ Objective

Students will read transition words, suggest words for a partner to include in his or her narrative, and write drafts of sentences for their own narratives using transition words.

## ➤ Introduction

*We will review transition words that authors use to show the passage of time and sequence of actions within an event in narrative writing. You will suggest words for a classmate to use in his or her writing and practice using words your classmate suggested for you.*

## ➤ Instruction

*We use transition words to help guide readers through the actions in a narrative event. Not every sentence needs transition words. The important thing is that the narrative flows naturally. In a narrative, transition words or phrases give readers a sense of time, since the things that happen within an experience are usually described in chronological order.*

## ➤ Guided Practice

Distribute "Narrative that Flows" (page 119) and student copies of "My Narrative Event Chart" (page 114). *Follow along as we read the transition words and phrases listed on "Narrative that Flows."* Discuss how these words and phrases guide readers through an event that is narrated in chronological order. *Why do we need transition words if the sentences are written in order?* (They can show the passage of time; for example, later, after a while, during, yesterday, before.) *Then read the actions your partner wrote on his or her copy of "My Narrative Event Chart." Next to each arrow on the chart (leading from one part of the experience to the next), write a transition word or phrase that might be appropriate.*

## ➤ Independent Practice

*Exchange papers so you have your original narrative event chart. Review the words and phrases your partner wrote on your chart on page 114. Then write sentences for your narrative on page 119 using the actions and transition words as appropriate.*

## ➤ Review

Review examples of effective use of transition words and phrases in print materials or student writing.

## ➤ Closing

*Today you practiced using transition words and phrases to connect events in your narrative.*

**Name(s):** _____

# Narrative that Flows

Read the actions your partner listed on his or her copy of "My Narrative Event Chart" (page 114). On each arrow of the chart between the actions that happen in the experience, write a transition word. Use the transition words below for ideas.

| | | | |
|---|---|---|---|
| about | after a while | as soon as | before |
| during | finally | immediately | later   next |
| since | soon | then | until   when |

Exchange papers and read the words and phrases your partner wrote on your event chart. Review the words and phrases discussed in class and decide which would be best for each major transition point in your narrative. You will not need transition words between every sentence; you want the sentences to flow naturally.

On the lines below, write sentences to describe the actions that happen in your narrative. Include one or more transition words suggested by your partner or from the words and phrases listed above.

_____

_____

_____

_____

_____

_____

_____

_____

_____

_____

_____

_____

_____

_____

_____

_____

_____

# Concluding Sentences

## ➤ Objective

Students will learn how to write a concluding sentence for a narrative paragraph and practice telling and writing sample concluding sentences for their narratives.

## ➤ Introduction

*Today you will identify a concluding sentence in a sample narrative, tell someone how your narrative ends, and write sample concluding sentences for your narratives.*

## ➤ Instruction

*The concluding sentence of a narrative paragraph wraps up the experience. Often the narrator may reflect on the impact of the experience and what he or she learned. After you've written most of your narrative, you might ask yourself, "Why did I choose to write about this experience, and why would readers want to read about it?"*

## ➤ Guided Practice

Display "A Logical Conclusion" (page 121). *How do you know which sentence introduces the narrative? Which transition words help you determine the order of actions within an event? Circle the transition words in the narrative. How do you know which sentence is the concluding sentence? Work with a partner to identify the concluding sentence and create a "What We Notice" chart about the concluding sentence. How will this activity help you when you write your narratives?* (We read what we write to make sure the actions within an event are described in an order that makes sense.)

## ➤ Independent Practice

Distribute "The End" (page 122). Share an example to model how to do Part One of the activity. For Part Two, prompt students to write one or two concluding sentences as if they were telling their narratives to someone.

## ➤ Review

Review ways students might conclude a narrative experience. Discuss possible alternate concluding sentences to the example paragraph on "A Logical Conclusion" as a review for students before they write their first drafts in the next lesson.

## ➤ Closing

*You discussed different ways to conclude a narrative experience and practiced sharing and writing sample concluding sentences for your narratives.*

## ➤ Answers

"A Logical Conclusion" (page 121): 1. The first sentence introduces the setting, narrator, and situation; 2. *Yesterday* tells when, *as* links ideas, *And* shows two ideas or actions that go together, *as* links the narrator's action and Ethan's action; 3. Sentence 13 concludes the narrative experience.

**Name(s):** _____

# A Logical Conclusion

Read the narrative paragraph. Then answer the questions below.

The hush of books holding their secrets and the scent of paper and ink greeted me as I tiptoed through the library yesterday to tackle our assigned task. We were to find interesting nonfiction books to read about topics we knew nothing about. That encompasses almost the entire nonfiction section, as I know nothing about museums, government, chemistry, or art. And I didn't want to read about supernatural stuff or the dictionary. We read plenty of myths and fairy tales and animal books in class. I sighed loudly. Ethan beckoned to me and said he'd show me the perfect book. I trailed behind him as he dashed to the transportation section and groaned because I did not want to read about rockets or trucks. I tried to face him directly but didn't succeed as he knelt down to peruse titles on the bottom shelf. He grasped a book and thrust it up at me. I turned the book over to read the title and inspect the cover photograph. It was a book on drones. I shrugged and carried my new learning adventure to the checkout desk.

1. How do you know which sentence is the topic sentence?

   _____

   _____

2. Which transition words help you determine the sequence of actions within an event?

   _____

   _____

3. How do you know which sentence is the concluding sentence?

   _____

   _____

4. Work with a partner to create a "What We Notice" chart about the concluding sentence. Use the back of this page.

---

### Teacher Notes

Grade level:  appropriate

Lexile estimate:  910L

---

Name(s): _____

# The End

## ➤ Part One

Work together with a partner to complete the activity below.

1.  Take turns sharing your narrative experience with a partner.

2.  Ask each other, "How did it end?"

3.  Write the ending your partner shared below.

_____

_____

_____

_____

_____

_____

_____

_____

## ➤ Part Two

Complete the activity below.

1.  Think about the narrative experience you plan to describe.

    •   How will your narrative end?

    •   What is the last thing that happens as part of this experience?

    •   What could you write that wraps up the experience and returns readers to their "ordinary" world?

2.  Write one or more sample concluding sentences for your narrative.

_____

_____

_____

_____

_____

_____

_____

_____

# First Draft and Peer Review

## ➤ Objective

Students will write first drafts of their narratives and participate in a peer-review activity to receive feedback on strengths and suggestions for areas that need improvement.

## ➤ Introduction

*Today you will compile your topic sentence, sentences describing the event in your narrative experience, and concluding sentence to write a first draft of your narrative paragraph. You will work with a small group to review each other's first drafts and offer feedback.*

## ➤ Instruction

*Often when we are ready to write a first draft, we already have an outline or notes about what we want to include in the narrative. You may need to brainstorm additional ideas and details about the topic, or the experience with drones you will describe. If possible, narrate the experience in first person to connect with readers. Use vivid descriptions to involve readers in the experience.*

## ➤ Guided Practice

*Refer to "My Narrative Event Chart" (page 114) to review the main event that happened as part of your experience. Decide who is telling about the experience—you or someone else. Use your notes from "Descriptive Details" (page 116) and "Narrative Action" (page 117) as you write.*

## ➤ Independent Practice

Group students with classmates to review students' first drafts of their narrative paragraphs. Distribute "Pre-flight Checklist" (page 124). *Take turns with others in your group reading the first drafts of your narrative paragraphs. Use this page to decide which narrative writer is the "expert" for each characteristic listed in the chart. Each narrative writer will be an expert in something, as everyone has strengths and weaknesses in their writing. Then discuss with your group ways in which you could improve your writing.*

## ➤ Review

Answer any questions as students write their first drafts. Assist students as needed to find at least one strength in each narrative draft within groups.

## ➤ Closing

*You have written a first draft of your narrative paragraph and received feedback on your writing from classmates.*

**Name(s):** _____

# Pre-flight Checklist

Work with a group to complete the activity below.

1.  Take turns reading your narrative paragraph to others in your group.

2.  Work together to decide which narrative paragraph has strengths in each area.

3.  Write each group member's name next to at least one characteristic; we all have strengths in some areas. Remember, writing does not have to be perfect to exhibit strengths in one or more areas of narrative writing.

| | | | | | |
|---|---|---|---|---|---|
| The narrative develops a real or imagined experience or event. | | | | | |
| The narrative has a topic sentence that introduces a narrator and a situation. | | | | | |
| The narrative uses descriptive words and sensory details to describe an experience or event. | | | | | |
| The narrative uses transition words and phrases to show a clear sequence of actions within an event. | | | | | |
| The narrative has a concluding sentence that flows naturally from the experience. | | | | | |

4.  Based on the feedback you receive in your group, discuss with classmates areas in which you would like to improve your writing.

5.  Ask "experts" in your group for ideas on how you can strengthen specific areas.

6.  Write notes below about the suggestions you receive.

_____

_____

_____

_____

_____

_____

_____

# Second Draft and Self-Evaluation

## ➤ Objective

Students will work with partners to identify areas for revision in their first drafts, write second drafts, and complete self-evaluations of their second drafts.

## ➤ Introduction

*You will use the notes from your first draft to write a second draft and then use a rubric to evaluate your writing.*

## ➤ Instruction

*The second draft gives writers the opportunity to continue to revise and make their writing stronger. One way to strengthen writing is to check grammar and sentence structure. Make sure sentences start in a variety of ways. This keeps your writing interesting for readers. Check for concrete words:  Does your writing have specific nouns that show readers exactly what you are writing about? Do you use precise adjectives to describe the nouns? Use adjectives only when necessary. Replace "to be" verbs with strong action words. Then check for any errors in spelling, punctuation, and capitalization.*

## ➤ Guided Practice

*Discuss with a partner specific things to revise in your first drafts. Help each other identify and strengthen sentence structure, word choice, and conventions. Use these notes along with your notes from "Pre-flight Checklist" (page 124) to write a second draft of your narrative.*

## ➤ Independent Practice

Distribute "Self-Evaluation:  Narrative Paragraph" (page 126). *Read each characteristic described on the page. Use different colors to highlight the sentence or sentences in the second draft of your narrative that correspond to each point on the rubric. Which score best describes that part of your narrative? Mark the score in the same color you used to highlight that characteristic on your paper (e.g., use blue to highlight the topic sentence in your paragraph and blue to mark your score for the first line of the rubric).*

## ➤ Review

Review and model the directions for Independent Practice as necessary to guide students through completing their self-evaluations.

## ➤ Closing

*You identified aspects of your first draft needing further revision, wrote a second draft, and used a rubric to evaluate your second draft.*

# Self-Evaluation: Narrative Paragraph

**Name:** _____    **Score:** _____

|  | **4** | **3** | **2** | **1** |
|---|---|---|---|---|
| **Topic Sentence** | My narrative has a topic sentence that establishes a situation and introduces a narrator and/or characters who had an experience with a drone. | My narrative has a topic sentence that introduces a narrator who had an experience with a drone. | My narrative has a topic sentence that introduces a character who narrates an experience. | My narrative does not have a topic sentence that establishes a situation or introduces the narrator. |
| **Experience/ Event** | My narrator describes an experience with a drone in an order that makes sense. | My narrator describes an experience with a drone. | My narrator describes an experience, but it is not told in an order that makes sense. | My narrative does not describe an experience. |
| **Descriptive Words and Actions** | I use descriptive words and multiple actions to describe an experience with a drone and to show how characters respond. | I use descriptive words and multiple actions to describe an experience with a drone. | I use descriptive words or multiple actions to describe an experience. | I do not use descriptive words or actions adequately to describe an experience. |
| **Details** | I include concrete words and sensory details to describe an experience with a drone. | I include concrete words or sensory details to describe an experience with a drone. | I include some details to describe an experience. | I do not include specific details to describe an experience. |
| **Transition Words** | I use transition words and phrases to guide readers through a logical sequence of actions within an experience. | I use transition words in some places to show the order of actions within an experience. | I use transition words once or twice to show the order of actions within an experience. | I do not use transition words to show the order of actions within an experience. |
| **Concluding Sentence** | My narrative has a concluding sentence that flows naturally from a narrated experience and provides a sense of closure. | My narrative has a concluding sentence that describes the end of an experience. | My narrative has a concluding sentence. | My narrative does not have a concluding sentence. |

# Final Draft

## ➤ Objective

Students will ask and answer questions as a whole group then write and review their final drafts.

## ➤ Introduction

*Today you will participate in a class discussion and use your self-evaluations to write and review the final draft of your narrative paragraph.*

## ➤ Instruction

*The final draft of a narrative piece is the copy we will present to an audience. We want our writing to be as clear as possible to make it easy for readers to understand. Think about the experience your narrative describes. Who would most enjoy reading it? A final draft represents writing that has been strengthened and improved through multiple revisions.*

## ➤ Guided Practice

*Review the scores you gave your narrative on "Self-Evaluation:  Narrative Paragraph" (page 126). Which parts of your narrative have lower scores? What are some questions you have about how to improve specific parts of a narrative paragraph?* Write student questions on a whiteboard or chart paper. Discuss possible answers together as a class. *Use your scored rubric and what you just heard in our class discussion to write a final draft of your narrative paragraph.*

## ➤ Independent Practice

Distribute "Ticket to the Finals" (page 128). *Review your final draft and complete the page to show your narrative is ready for an audience. Compare your final draft to your first draft and answer the questions to reflect on your writing process and learning.*

## ➤ Review

Check students' work ("Ticket to the Finals"). Discuss potential audiences with students together as a class or in small groups.

## ➤ Closing

*You reviewed the scores from your self-evaluation and asked and answered questions with classmates about how to make final revisions to a narrative paragraph. You wrote the final draft of your narrative paragraph and reviewed it to compare it with your first draft.*

Name(s): _____

# Ticket to the Finals

## ➤ Part One

Review your final draft for each qualification listed below. When applicable, put checkmarks in the tickets.

My draft has features of strong narrative writing.

I used a variety of sentence structures and descriptive words.

I checked my writing for correct spelling, punctuation, capitalization, and grammar.

My draft is ready to go. I will present it to _____.
                                                                        *(audience)*

## ➤ Part Two

Compare your first draft with your final draft. Then answer the questions below.

1. What changes did you make?

   _____

   _____

   _____

2. Why did you make those changes?

   _____

   _____

   _____

3. In what ways is your final draft stronger than your first draft?

   _____

   _____

   _____

4. In what ways is your final draft now ready for your audience?

   _____

   _____

# Final Evaluation

## ➤ Objective

Students will participate in an introductory class discussion and then compare the feedback and scores their narrative paragraphs received throughout the drafting and revising process. They will reflect on the scores they received to identify areas of strength and one target area for improvement in the next narrative writing module.

## ➤ Introduction

*Today you will use a visual aid to compare feedback you received from classmates and me, as well as the scores you gave your writing on your self-evaluation. Then you will answer questions to reflect on your observations.*

## ➤ Instruction

*People use visuals to see data at a glance.* Display a sample donut chart. *This type of chart is one way to visually compare data in similar categories from different sources. When you compare feedback you receive on your writing from classmates, your own self-evaluation, and the scores you receive from me, you are comparing data in the same categories (characteristics of effective narrative writing) from different sources.*

## ➤ Guided Practice

*Think back to classmates' drafts you reviewed on "Pre-flight Checklist" (page 124). Which students had strengths in each area? How do you think your small group would have scored your narrative for each characteristic?* Distribute "Graphing My Scores" (page 130). *Each circle has a segment for each characteristic listed on the rubric we used to evaluate your narrative paragraph. The inner circle represents the scores you think you might have received from classmates in your small group, based on what you remember of the discussion. Write the score you think you might have received from your small group for each characteristic.* Distribute completed evaluations ("Self-Evaluation: Narrative Paragraph" [page 126] and "Teacher Evaluation:  Narrative Paragraph" [page 131]) to each student. *In the second circle, write the scores you gave yourself on the self-evaluation. In the outer circle, write the scores you received on the teacher evaluation. The solid center circle will remain blank.*

## ➤ Independent Practice

*Review the similarities and differences in the feedback and scores your narrative writing received during the process of drafting and revising. Reflect on ways in which your writing improved and identify one characteristic you would like to focus on and strengthen in the next narrative writing module.*

## ➤ Review

Assist students in recalling and reviewing small group discussions and feedback from the "Pre-flight Checklist" activity.

## ➤ Closing

*You recalled a small-group discussion, reviewed scores you gave your narrative writing, and compared them to the evaluation I gave your narrative paragraph.*

Name(s): _____

# Graphing My Scores

➤ **Part One**

Compare the feedback and evaluations you received on your writing from a small-group discussion, your self-evaluation, and the teacher's evaluation of your final narrative. In the inner circle, write the scores you think you might have received from your small group. In the second circle, write the scores you gave yourself on the self-evaluation. In the outer circle, write the scores you received on the teacher evaluation.

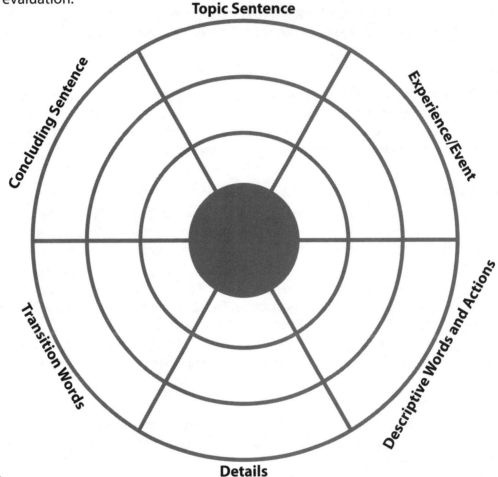

➤ **Part Two**

Complete the following sentence frames.

1. When my small group completed "Pre-flight Checklist" (page 124), my writing showed strength

   in _____.

2. When I completed the "Self-Evaluation: Narrative Paragraph" (page 126), my scores showed my

   narrative had _____.

3. On the "Teacher Evaluation: Narrative Paragraph" (page 131), the scores I received showed my

   strengths are _____.

4. I would like to keep improving my writing to become an expert in _____

   _____.

# Teacher Evaluation: Narrative Paragraph

**Student Name:** _____    **Score:** _____

|  | 4 | 3 | 2 | 1 |
|---|---|---|---|---|
| **Topic Sentence** | The narrative has a topic sentence that establishes a situation and introduces a narrator and/or characters who had an experience with a drone. | The narrative has a topic sentence that introduces a narrator who had an experience with a drone. | The narrative has a topic sentence that introduces a character who narrates an experience. | The narrative does not have a topic sentence that introduces the narrator or any characters. |
| **Experience/ Event** | The narrator describes an experience with a drone in an order that makes sense. | The narrator describes an experience with a drone. | The narrator describes an experience, but it is not told in an order that makes sense. | The narrative does not describe an experience. |
| **Descriptive Words and Actions** | The author uses descriptive words and multiple actions to describe an experience with a drone and to show how characters respond. | The author uses descriptive words and multiple actions to describe an experience with a drone. | The author uses descriptive words or multiple actions to describe an experience. | The author does not use descriptive words or actions adequately to describe an experience. |
| **Details** | The author includes concrete words and sensory details to describe an experience with a drone. | The author includes concrete words or sensory details to describe an experience with a drone. | The author includes some details to describe an experience. | The author does not include specific details to describe an experience. |
| **Transition Words** | The author uses transition words and phrases to guide readers through a logical sequence of actions within an experience. | The author uses transition words in some places to show the order of actions within an experience. | The author uses transition words once or twice to show the order of actions within an experience. | The author does not use transition words to show the order of actions within an experience. |
| **Concluding Sentence** | The narrative has a concluding sentence that flows naturally from a narrated experience and provides a sense of closure. | The narrative has a concluding sentence that describes the end of an experience. | The narrative has a concluding sentence. | The narrative does not have a satisfactory concluding sentence. |

# Review

## ➤ Objective

Students will read narrative examples and identify characteristics of narrative writing. They will practice rewriting a narrative paragraph to strengthen it.

## ➤ Introduction

*You have written your own narrative paragraph. Today you will read narrative samples and identify characteristics of narrative writing, and then rewrite one sample to strengthen the writing.*

## ➤ Instruction

*Narrative writing describes a real or imagined experience by conveying a clear sequence of actions within an event using descriptive details. It has a topic sentence that introduces a narrator and establishes a setting and context for the story. Concrete words and sensory details invite readers to experience the event along with the narrator. It includes transition words that indicate the passage of time and guide readers through the actions. A satisfactory concluding sentence ends the experience in a way that makes sense based on the event that happened.*

## ➤ Guided Practice

Distribute "Drones for Everyone" (page 133). *Refer to a list of characteristics of narrative writing, such as "Characteristics of a Narrative Paragraph" (page 106), "Pre-flight Checklist" (page 124), or "Self-Evaluation: Narrative Paragraph" (page 126) to complete "Drones for Everyone." In the margins of the narrative, write the different characteristics you notice. Draw an arrow from each speech bubble to the corresponding sentence in the sample.*

## ➤ Independent Practice

*Think about what you have learned about narrative writing.* Distribute "View from a Drone: A Review of Narrative Writing" (page 134). *Answer the questions in Part One and then read the narrative sample in Part Two. On the back of the page, rewrite the narrative, incorporating elements of strong narrative writing.*

## ➤ Review

Review "Drones for Everyone" with students, discussing appropriate responses. Discuss the quality of the sample on "View from a Drone: A Review of Narrative Writing" and possible responses. Invite volunteers to read their rewritten narratives.

## ➤ Closing

*You have reviewed the characteristics of narrative writing and identified these qualities in sample narratives. You used what you have learned about writing narratives to strengthen and rewrite a sample narrative.*

## ➤ Answers

"Drones for Everyone" (page 133): Accept reasonable answers.

"View from a Drone: A Review of Narrative Writing" (page 134): *Part One*—1. It is writing that uses descriptive details and a clear action sequence to tell about a narrator's experience; 2. concrete words; sensory details; transition words; introduction of narrator, situation, and setting; satisfying concluding sentence; *Part Two*—1. setting is unclear, narrative needs more descriptive words and sensory details, sequence of actions within the event is unclear and lacking transition words, concluding sentence is vague; 2. It describes a narrator's experience with interactions between characters and a few details about the actions within an event.

# Drones for Everyone

I stretched tall in my seat to see the stage over the heads of the first graders in the first row. The room hummed with the voices of hundreds of kids. Everyone waited for the assembly to begin. For days, I'd been looking forward to watching this drone demonstration. I nudged Keira, who sat next to me, and leaned over the armrest of the seats. I asked her if she thought we would really get drones in our classroom. She shook her head, and then she perked up a little and craned her neck to see the stage. Two or three tables sat on the stage draped with heavy black cloths. Mrs. Rivas stepped to the center of the stage and waited for everyone to settle down. The vice principal walked toward the table that had the smaller drone. Mrs. Rivas whisked the cloths away with a flourish. Then the principal picked up the controller for the machine. He explained how kids could use drones to study natural disasters and how they affect people. Using the controls, he demonstrated the drone flying to and hovering over a partially dismantled building block scene. He said that drones fly into dangerous situations. They take photographs to inform police and others of the amount of damage so people can plan relief efforts. That sounded pretty good to me. After further demonstrations, we went back to class. I told Keira I couldn't wait to build my own drone with my grandpa. We would use spare parts and attach an old camera. Keira laughed and teased that I would save the world.

## Teacher Notes

Grade level:  appropriate

Lexile estimate:  820L

**Name(s):** _____

# View from a Drone:  A Review of Narrative Writing

## ➤ Part One

Based on what you know about narrative writing, answer the following questions.

**1.** What is narrative writing? How would you define a narrative?

_____

_____

**2.** What other qualities does a strong narrative have?

_____

_____

**3.** What is one thing you have learned about narrative writing?

_____

## ➤ Part Two

Read the sample narrative. Then answer the questions below.

Dad shook his finger at me as if he might forbid me from attending school ever again. He told me that drones were dangerous and should not be used in the classroom. My teacher had sent a note home that day explaining that our class would have the opportunity to participate in a drone activity the next day. I reminded him that quadcopters weren't good or bad. It was all in how people used them. Mom reassured Dad that I wouldn't pilot a drone and that I would follow all the safety rules. She looked directly at me as she said the last part. I nodded my head vigorously. Mom and Dad's agreement to my participation was the first step toward me eventually being able to purchase my own drone—I hoped.

**1.** What is missing from this narrative?

_____

_____

**2.** What makes this writing sample a narrative?

_____

_____

**3.** On the back of this page, rewrite this narrative, incorporating elements of strong narrative writing.

---

**Teacher Notes**

Grade level:  appropriate

Lexile estimate:  860L

---

# Introductory Paragraphs

## ➤ Objective

Students will work in small groups to brainstorm ideas for their narrative essays. They will also discuss ways authors begin a narrative and study opening lines from classic works. After researching weather, students will draft descriptive sentences related to their narratives.

## ➤ Introduction

*In this module, you will plan and write a narrative about an experience you or a character has had observing weather and its effect on people or nature. Your narrative will begin with an introductory paragraph that contains a thesis statement. Today you will brainstorm ideas about the narrator, setting, and context of your narrative. You will examine different ways authors begin a story and consider the effect weather has on people, places, and events.*

## ➤ Instruction

*In a narrative essay, the introductory paragraph has a thesis statement. The thesis statement introduces the setting and context of the situation, including the narrator and characters involved. It is important to introduce the story in an interesting way to catch readers' attention so they will want to keep reading.*

## ➤ Guided Practice

Distribute "Building a Narrative" (page 136). *You will work with a small group to brainstorm ideas for the introductory paragraph of your narrative essay. You will each complete the graphic on this page for the narrator or main character of your essay, with assistance from group members. Brainstorm information about the experience your narrative will describe: details about related events, other people who were there, and the setting. When you consider setting, think about the time of day or time of year, the weather, and the place.*

Distribute "Beginnings" (page 137) and discuss the list of techniques authors use to start a narrative. *Work with a partner to read sample opening lines from famous books. Decide which technique each example demonstrates and write it on the lines below the quote. Then discuss and answer the questions about ways to begin a narrative.*

## ➤ Independent Practice

Distribute "Weather Report" (page 138). *With your partner, research to learn about the weather for the place and time of year that relates to your narrative experience. Complete the chart using the example as a guide. Then use the sample opening lines from "Beginnings" as models and write several sentences that might be part of an introductory paragraph for your essay. Incorporate the ideas you brainstormed with your small group, as well as details you learned about the weather for your story.*

## ➤ Review

Review the techniques used in the sample opening lines and prompt students to recall other openings in books they have read that refer to weather to introduce a setting and narrative context.

## ➤ Closing

*You brainstormed ideas for introducing the narrator, setting, and context of your narrative and thought about the role weather might play.*

## ➤ Answers

"Beginnings" (page 137): 1. Create drama; 2. Use sensory or descriptive details to introduce the setting; 3. Use figurative language; 4. Get right into the story; 5. Use sensory or descriptive details to introduce the setting and character; 6. Use descriptive details to introduce the character and story situation.

Name(s): _____

# Building a Narrative

Write the name of the narrator or main character for your narrative essay on the girl's shirt.

With others in your group, brainstorm details about the experience your character will describe. Include other people who were there, the setting, and the actions within the experience. When you consider setting, think about the time of day or time of year, the weather, and the place.

Answer the questions below to help you think about the narrative experience. Write your answers on a separate piece of paper.

- What was the weather like?
- How did the weather affect the experience/events?
- What happened?
- How did the narrator or main character respond?
- What would have changed if the weather had been different?

Refer to your responses to write details about the narrative in the speech bubbles above.

# Beginnings

## ➤ Part One

Study the following ways an author might choose to begin a narrative:

- Use sensory or descriptive details to introduce the character, setting, and/or story situation.
- Start with dialogue.
- Create drama.
- Use figurative language (e.g., metaphor, onomatopoeia).
- Get right into the story.

## ➤ Part Two

With a partner, read the following opening lines from famous books. On the lines below each quote, write the technique the author used.

1. "It was the best of times, it was the worst of times, it was the season of Light, it was the season of Darkness, it was the spring of hope, it was the winter of despair."

   _____

2. "It was a dark and stormy night. The rain fell in torrents, halted occasionally by a violent gust of wind which swept up the streets. It rattled along the house tops and disturbed the flame of the lamps struggling against the darkness."

   _____

3. "The cold passed reluctantly from the earth, and the retiring fogs revealed an army stretched out on the hills, resting."

   _____

4. "The sun did not shine, it was too wet to play, so we sat in the house all that cold, cold wet day. I sat there with Sally. We sat here we two and we said 'How we wish we had something to do.'"

   _____

5. "Once on a dark winter's day, when the yellow fog hung so thick and heavy in the streets of London that the lamps were lighted and the shop windows blazed with gas as they do at night, an odd-looking little girl sat in a cab with her father and was driven rather slowly through the big thoroughfares."

   _____

6. "It was so glorious out in the country; it was summer; the cornfields were yellow, the oats were green, the hay had been put up in stacks in the green meadows, and the stork went about on his long red legs, and chattered Egyptian, for this was the language he had learned from his good mother."

   _____

## ➤ Part Three

Use the back of this page to answer the questions below.

1. Which techniques were most effective?

2. How can referring to the weather introduce setting and context for a narrative?

Name(s): _____

# Weather Report

Use weather sites, newspapers, weather apps, and other print and online resources to research the weather. Focus on the location of your narrative experience and the time of year the events take place. Fill out the chart below, using the example as a guide.

Example:

| Sky Condition | showers likely |
|---|---|
| High Temperature | 68°F |
| Low Temperature | 56°F |
| % Chance of Precipitation | 70% chance showers |
| Wind | WSW 5 MPH |

| Sky Condition | |
|---|---|
| High Temperature | |
| Low Temperature | |
| % Chance of Precipitation | |
| Wind | |

Using this page and "Beginnings" (page 137), write several sentences to describe the weather in your narrative, including as many sensory details as possible. Include one or two sentences about how the weather will affect the narrator, another character, the events in the experience, or the setting.

_____

_____

_____

_____

_____

_____

_____

_____

_____

_____

_____

# Body Paragraphs

## ➤ Objective

Students will discuss actions and responses people demonstrate in various situations involving weather.

## ➤ Introduction

*Today you will participate in a class discussion about how people respond and act in different types of weather, and draw pictures to show dialogue and action. You will also outline the events that happen in the experience you will describe in your narrative essay and practice writing sentences about those events with transition words.*

## ➤ Instruction

*People respond in different ways to things that happen to them. Characters react by talking or acting. Authors use dialogue and concrete words to show speech and action in a narrative. Descriptive words that involve the senses help readers envision the details of the setting and event. Authors use transition words in narratives to show the passage of time. Transition words can also show characters moving from one place to another. These words and phrases connect events in an experience in a logical order and help readers follow the action.*

## ➤ Guided Practice

As a class, discuss what students do in different types of weather. Conduct a role-play activity and prompt students to demonstrate their actions and responses in various weather-related situations. Distribute "Rain or Shine (page 140). Prompt #1: *What do you do when you are in the middle of an activity and the weather changes?* Prompt #2: *How do people's actions and reactions differ if the weather changes from good to bad or from bad to good?* Discuss descriptive words and sensory details students could incorporate into their writing, using a thesaurus as a resource. Have students complete Part Two independently.

## ➤ Independent Practice

Distribute "Steps in Your Experience" (page 141). *Think about the events that are part of the experience you will narrate. What happened first? What happened last? Write each event on its own step, in the order in which it happened. Include the most important parts of the experience that you will write about in your narrative essay. Then use the words in the word box, or other appropriate transition words and phrases, to write sentences about the events.*

## ➤ Review

Review student work from "Steps in Your Experience" for appropriate use of transition words.

## ➤ Closing

*You considered character actions in response to a situation and practiced writing dialogue and using transition words.*

Name(s): _____

# Rain or Shine

## ➤ Part One

Participate in the class discussion and observe classmates' actions and responses to weather prompts. Then write words, including sensory details, to describe the situations.

Prompt #1: _____

_____

_____

Prompt #2: _____

_____

_____

## ➤ Part Two

Think about the situations you discussed with classmates. Draw pictures in the boxes below to show how weather affects an experience. In your drawing, include dialogue and actions to show how the characters react in the situation.

| | | |
|---|---|---|
| | | |
| | | |

# Steps in Your Experience

## ➤ Part One

On the steps below, write events that happened during your narrative experience in order. List only the most important parts that you will include in your narrative.

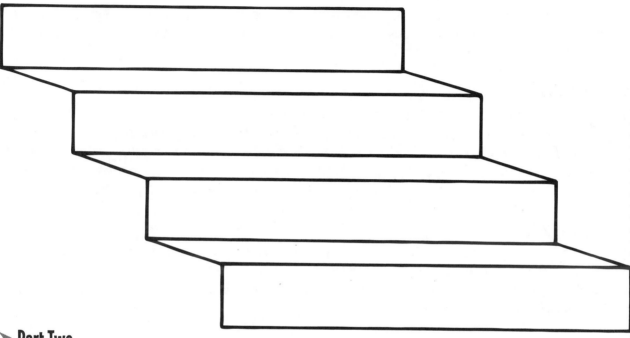

## ➤ Part Two

Use transition words or phrases from the word bank below to write sentences about the events in your narrative experience. Include other transition words as needed or appropriate.

| | | |
|---|---|---|
| a few days after | but | in front of |
| another | by the time | so |
| as | for a while | the next day |
| at that moment | however | when |

_____

_____

_____

_____

_____

_____

# Conclusions

## ➤ Objective

Students will discuss possible ways to end a narrative, receive suggestions from partners, answer reflective questions, and draft conclusions for their narratives.

## ➤ Introduction

*Today you will work with a partner to discuss ways to end a narrative. You will also answer thinking questions and use your responses, along with suggestions you receive from your partner, to write a sample conclusion for your narrative.*

## ➤ Instruction

*Effective narrative writing gives readers a powerful emotional experience. This means what happened to the characters in the narrative influences the reader in some way. The conclusion in a narrative essay brings the experience to a close. It's important to allow readers to come to their own conclusions. The narrator may reflect on how this experience changed the way he or she thinks or will do things in the future. Alternatively, the ending of a narrative essay may impact readers in some way by including a thought to ponder or a lesson learned from the experience.*

## ➤ Guided Practice

Distribute "In Conclusion" (page 143). *Authors use a variety of methods to end a narrative. Discuss the suggestions on this page with a partner. How might each option apply to your narrative? Brainstorm possible conclusions using each technique. Suggest one or two options for your partner to try with his or her narrative. Respond both verbally and in writing to your partner's suggestion.*

## ➤ Independent Practice

Distribute "Powerful Endings" (page 144). *Read these questions and reflect on the experience you described in your narrative. Answer the questions and then consider your responses. Use your insights from answering these questions along with the suggestions you received from your partner on "In Conclusion" to write a sample conclusion for your narrative.*

## ➤ Review

Review the tips for ending a narrative on "In Conclusion," offering print, online, or student-generated examples of each tip.

## ➤ Closing

*Today you thought about how to write a conclusion for your narrative by discussing tips with a partner and answering questions about your narrative.*

**Name(s):** _____

# In Conclusion

## ➤ Part One

The following are tips for how to end a narrative. Read and then discuss with a classmate.

- Use descriptive words to paint a mental picture.
- End with a specific action.
- If characters speak in the narrative, it's possible to end with dialogue.
- Offer a thought about what happened.
- Share what you or your narrator learned or realized as a result of the experience.
- Reflect on the experience so your readers will also reflect.

## ➤ Part Two

Trade papers. Suggest one or more tips that might be helpful for your partner to use in his or her conclusion. Complete the following sentence frame.

I think you could try ending your narrative with _____ because

_____

_____

_____

_____.

Return your partner's paper to him or her. Now write a response to your partner's suggestion.

_____

_____

_____

_____

_____

_____

_____

_____

_____

_____

_____

_____

**Name(s):** _____

# Powerful Endings

## ➤ Part One

Consider what makes an effective conclusion. Answer the questions below.

**1.** What happened at the end of your experience?

_____

_____

**2.** What did you or the narrator learn or discover by going through this experience?

_____

_____

**3.** How did this experience change the way you or the narrator thinks or behaves?

_____

_____

**4.** How might this experience influence your readers?

_____

_____

**5.** What might readers reflect on or learn as a result of reading your narrative?

_____

_____

**6.** What made this experience important?

_____

_____

## ➤ Part Two

Write a sample conclusion using the tips your partner gave you and your answers above.

_____

_____

_____

_____

_____

# First Draft and Peer Review

## ➤ Objective

Students will use a graphic to guide them through the process of writing first drafts of their narrative essays and then read their drafts aloud to classmates as part of a peer-review activity.

## ➤ Introduction

*Today you will write the first draft of your narrative essay. Then you will read your writing aloud to a partner and participate in a peer-review activity.*

## ➤ Instruction

*When an author writes a first draft, he or she puts all his or her notes and ideas together into one complete narrative, in order from introduction to conclusion. In your first draft, you will put your notes and practice sentences from activities in previous lessons together to write your narrative essay. Your draft will include an introductory paragraph, in which you introduce a narrator, situation, and setting in a thesis statement. The body paragraphs will describe the events that were part of the narrative experience, in the order they happened. You will use concrete words and sensory details to describe the experience, and dialogue and actions to show how characters reacted to what happened. And, finally, you will write a conclusion that ends the narrative in a way that makes sense and leaves readers with something to think about.*

## ➤ Guided Practice

Distribute "Making Connections" (page 146). *Match each part of a narrative essay with its description in Part One of "Making Connections." Use the guide below in Part Two to write your rough draft. Gather your notes and ideas from the activities mentioned and color each icon as you write that part of your narrative.*

## ➤ Independent Practice

*Read your first draft aloud to a classmate. After you read, review the parts of a narrative essay described in Part One of "Making Connections." Notice areas in which you'd like to make changes and mark those places. Offer and receive feedback from your partner about parts that need strengthening and make additional notes.*

## ➤ Review

Review the parts of a narrative as outlined on "Making Connections" and review characteristics of each.

## ➤ Closing

*You wrote the first draft of your narrative essay and read it aloud to a partner to consider areas in which you'd like to make changes when you write your second draft.*

## ➤ Answers

"Making Connections" (page 146):  Introductory Paragraph—A, E, G; Body Paragraphs—B, D, F; Conclusion—C

# Making Connections

## ➤ Part One

Read the list of writing tasks and purposes that are part of a narrative essay. Write each one in the appropriate column of the chart below to show where in the essay each part belongs.

(**A**) Establishes a situation

(**B**) Consist of events that are part of the experience

(**C**) Flows naturally from a described experience

(**D**) Includes concrete words and sensory details to describe experiences and events

(**E**) Describes a setting

(**F**) Uses dialogue and actions to show character responses to events

(**G**) Introduces a narrator

| Introductory Paragraph | Body Paragraphs | Conclusion |
|---|---|---|
|  |  |  |

## ➤ Part Two

Use the guide below to write your rough draft. Gather your notes and ideas from the activities mentioned and color each icon as you write that part of your narrative.

**Introductory Paragraph**

Building a Narrative (page 136)

Weather Report (page 138)

**Body Paragraphs**

Rain or Shine (page 140)

Steps in Your Experience (page 141)

**Conclusion**

In Conclusion (page 143)

Powerful Endings (page 144)

# Second Draft and Self-Evaluation

## ➤ Objective

Students will write second drafts of their narrative essays, evaluate their drafts using a rubric, and identify areas to strengthen when writing their final drafts.

## ➤ Introduction

*Today you will write the second draft of your narrative essay, using notes from your peer review. You will score your writing using a rubric and mark areas you would like to strengthen when you write your final draft.*

## ➤ Instruction

*Think about the qualities of effective narrative writing as you write the second draft of your narrative essay. Include specific descriptions of people, places, and things to give readers a mental picture of the experience. Use sensory details; for example, describe what a character sees, hears, or smells. Show readers what the character encounters and how he or she reacts to events in the experience. Consider using metaphors and similes to make your writing more interesting. Check the progression of events in your narrative, and fill in any gaps with details as needed.*

## ➤ Guided Practice

*Review your first draft and the notes you made when meeting with a classmate. Check your introductory paragraph. Which sentence would most grab readers' attention? You might need to rearrange your sentences to hook the reader. Read your body paragraphs and check the dialogue, action, and details you used to describe your experience. Review your conclusion and the overall impact your narrative will have on readers. Write a second draft using your notes to strengthen your essay based on these suggestions.*

## ➤ Independent Practice

Distribute "Self-Evaluation: Narrative Essay" (page 148). *Evaluate your second draft using this rubric. Circle or highlight the score that best describes your writing for each part of your narrative. Identify areas you would like to strengthen when you write your final draft, and underline or highlight those sentences. On the back of the self-evaluation, write notes about how you will improve your writing.*

## ➤ Review

Review "Self-Evaluation: Narrative Essay" with students and answer any questions about the rubric. Discuss how students can use the characteristics described on the rubric to identify areas they would like to strengthen when they write their final drafts.

## ➤ Closing

*You used a rubric to evaluate your second draft and took notes about things you would like to strengthen in your writing. Use the scores on your rubric and your notes to write a final draft of your narrative. Type your final copy, if possible, and bring it back to class for the next lesson.*

# Self-Evaluation: Narrative Essay

**Name:** _____   **Score:** _____

| | 4 | 3 | 2 | 1 |
|---|---|---|---|---|
| **Narrator and/or Character(s)** | My narrative introduces a narrator and/or characters who had a weather-related experience, in an interesting way. | My narrative introduces a narrator and/or characters who had a weather-related experience. | My narrative introduces a character who narrates an experience. | My narrative does not introduce the narrator or any characters. |
| **Situation and Setting** | My narrative introduces a setting and situation about weather to orient my readers. | My narrative introduces a situation about weather. | My narrative introduces a setting, but the situation is unclear. | My narrative does not introduce a setting or a situation. |
| **Experience(s)/ Event(s)** | My narrator describes events in a weather-related experience in an order that makes sense. | My narrator describes events in a weather-related experience. | My narrator describes weather-related events in an order that doesn't make sense. | My narrative does not describe weather-related events. |
| **Dialogue and Description** | I use dialogue and description to describe a weather-related experience and to show how characters respond. | I use dialogue and description to describe a weather-related experience. | I use dialogue or description to describe an experience. | I do not use dialogue or description adequately to describe an experience. |
| **Details** | I include concrete words and sensory details to describe events in my narrative about a weather-related experience. | I include concrete words or sensory details to describe events in my narrative about a weather-related experience. | I include details to describe events in my narrative. | I do not include specific details to describe events in my narrative. |
| **Transition Words** | I use transition words and phrases to guide readers through the sequence of events. | I use transition words in some places to show the order of events. | I use transition words once or twice to show the order of events. | I do not use transition words to show the order of events. |
| **Conclusion** | My narrative has a conclusion that flows naturally from the narrated experience and provides a sense of closure. | My narrative has a conclusion that describes the end of an experience. | My narrative has a conclusion. | My narrative does not have a satisfactory conclusion. |

148

# Review

## ➤ Objective

Students will read and analyze a narrative essay, answering and discussing questions in small groups. Then they will further consider the narrative by completing prompts and suggesting ways to strengthen the writing.

## ➤ Introduction

*Now that you have written a narrative essay, you will read and examine a sample narrative. With a small group, you will answer and discuss questions about the essay and then reflect on the author's writing and ways it could be strengthened.*

## ➤ Instruction

*One way to learn about specific types of writing is to study models. You have learned about the characteristics of narrative writing, or specific things to notice in this type of writing. Read the sample narrative with the categories from the scoring rubrics in mind to identify ways the author included these qualities in his or her writing.*

## ➤ Guided Practice

Distribute "Caught in a Squall" (page 150) and "Narrative Writing:  Another Look" (page 151). *Work with a small group to read this narrative essay. Then answer the questions in Part One of "Narrative Writing:  Another Look." Discuss your responses to the questions with others in the group.*

## ➤ Independent Practice

*Work on your own to complete Part Two of "Narrative Writing:  Another Look." What did you learn about narrative writing from reading this essay? How would you change the narrative and why?*

## ➤ Review

Review the categories described on "Self-Evaluation:  Narrative Essay" (page 148) and discuss how the narrative exemplified the characteristics of narrative writing.

## ➤ Closing

*You read a sample narrative essay about a weather-related experience and studied how the author used characteristics of narrative writing for effect. You discussed specific parts of the essay with classmates in a small group and considered ways the writing could be strengthened.*

## ➤ Answers

"Narrative Writing:  Another Look" (page 151):  Part One—1. One spring morning, I walked on the beach with my family; 2. beach; stated by narrator and described with words such as surf, shells, waves, etc.; 3. a storm; 4. crashing, soared, quickened, surge, swell, descended, downpour, pounded, tackled, particles, blasted, soaking, driving, huddle, blanketing, refuge, narrow, staggered, dense, collapsed, shone, sparkled; 5. Answers will vary. Part Two—The narrative describes the experience of being caught in a sudden squall; Answers will vary.

# Caught in a Squall

One spring morning, I walked on the beach with my family. I loved to watch the crashing surf. Seagulls soared and dove as we searched for shells and agates. Normally we would also watch other people out on the beach, but there weren't many today. To the west, clouds began to build and grow dark. It looked like a fast rising storm, so we quickened our pace and turned back towards our motel room.

As soon as we started back, the waves began to surge and swell. The sky grew black as a wall of clouds gathered and descended upon us.

At first, the rain was soft, and the wind blowing in our faces seemed more like a strong breeze. Within minutes, the downpour became heavier. Large raindrops pounded us as the wind blew our hoods back. We struggled in vain to keep them up.

Before we could get even a few blocks back toward safety, a full-force storm tackled us. The raindrops turned to ice particles and blew in our faces. Gusts of wind blasted wet sand straight at us and over the tops of our heads.

The stinging ice particles and cold winds continued to gust upwards of 40 miles per hour. As wet, driving sand covered our faces and clung to our soaking clothes, walking came to a halt. Our lungs became heavy with cold air, and we could hardly draw the next breath.

Finally, with no strength to move forward, we wondered if we should huddle on the beach with sand blanketing us and wait for the squall to pass. We chose to walk up toward the street to find refuge. Finding a narrow opening, we staggered through the dense sand, across sand grass, and then between houses. We collapsed in the shelter of a multi-story building and waited for the storm to blow over.

And so it did within minutes. The sun shone through a break in the clouds and sparkled on the ocean, as if nothing had happened.

> **Teacher Notes**
>
> Grade level:  appropriate
> Lexile estimate:  880L

**Name(s):** _____

# Narrative Writing: Another Look

## ➤ Part One

Read "Caught in a Squall " (page 150) and discuss the narrative and the following questions with a small group.

**1.** Which sentence or sentences introduce the narrator?

_____

_____

**2.** What is the setting of the narrative? How do you know?

_____

_____

**3.** Based on the introductory paragraph, what do you expect to happen in the narrative?

_____

**4.** What concrete words and sensory details does the author use to describe events and experiences?

_____

_____

_____

**5.** How does the description and action contribute to your understanding of the experience?

_____

_____

## ➤ Part Two

Complete the following sentence frames on your own.

• The narrative describes the experience of _____.

• Other characters in the narrative responded to events by _____

_____.

• As a result of reading this essay, I learned _____.

• The author showed excellence in his or her writing by _____

_____.

• This essay could be improved by _____

_____.

# Final Evaluation

## ➤ Objective

Students will compare their self-evaluation scores with their teacher-evaluation scores on their narrative essays from this module. They will then answer reflective questions about their learning and writing progress.

## ➤ Introduction

*Today you will compare the scores you gave your narrative essay about a weather-related experience with the scores I gave your writing.*

## ➤ Instruction

*We can use rubrics to observe our writing progress in specific areas over time. During the last two modules, you have learned about and practiced writing narratives. Narrative writing has distinctive characteristics:  a narrator, a situation, a setting, a description of an experience that includes events that happen in sequential order and sensory details, and an ending that concludes the narrative and reflects on the impact of the experience on the narrator and readers. When we compare scores from essays we wrote at different times, we see areas in which we have strengthened our writing.*

## ➤ Guided Practice

Distribute copies of "My Writing Progress" (page 154) and the second and final drafts of students' weather-related narrative essays, along with student copies of "Self-Evaluation:  Narrative Essay" (page 148) and "Teacher Evaluation: Narrative Essay" (page 153). *Reread both essays you have written and review the scores you received on each. Enter the scores in the appropriate boxes in the chart on page 154.*

## ➤ Independent Practice

*Answer the questions below the chart to reflect on your writing progress. Conference with me or a classmate to discuss what you have learned about narrative writing.*

## ➤ Review

Review the categories for scoring on the "Teacher Evaluation:  Narrative Essay" and clarify or answer questions as needed.

## ➤ Closing

*Today you compared the scores you gave your narrative essay on a weather-related experience with the scores you received from me. You considered changes in the scores and reflected on your progress in narrative writing.*

# Teacher Evaluation: Narrative Essay

**Student Name:** _____        Score: _____

|  | 4 | 3 | 2 | 1 |
|---|---|---|---|---|
| **Narrator and/or Character(s)** | The narrative introduces a narrator and/or characters who had a weather-related experience, in an interesting way. | The narrative introduces a narrator and/or characters who had a weather-related experience. | The narrative introduces a character who narrates an experience. | The narrative does not introduce the narrator or any characters. |
| **Situation and Setting** | The narrative introduces a setting and situation about weather to orient readers. | The narrative introduces a situation about weather. | The narrative introduces a setting, but the situation is unclear. | The narrative does not introduce a setting or a situation. |
| **Experience(s)/ Event(s)** | The narrator describes events in the weather-related experience in an order that makes sense. | The narrator describes events in the weather-related experience. | The narrator describes weather-related events in an order that doesn't make sense. | The narrative does not describe weather-related events. |
| **Dialogue and Description** | The author uses dialogue and description to describe a weather-related experience and to show how characters respond. | The author uses dialogue and description to describe a weather-related experience. | The author uses dialogue or description to describe an experience. | The author does not use dialogue or description adequately to describe an experience. |
| **Details** | The author includes concrete words and sensory details to describe events in the narrative about a weather-related experience. | The author includes concrete words or sensory details to describe events in the narrative about a weather-related experience. | The author includes details to describe events in the narrative. | The author does not include specific details to describe events in the narrative. |
| **Transition Words** | The author uses transition words and phrases to guide readers through the sequence of events. | The author uses transition words in some places to show the order of events. | The author uses transition words once or twice to show the order of events. | The author does not use transition words to show the order of events. |
| **Conclusion** | The narrative has a conclusion that flows naturally from the narrated experience and provides a sense of closure. | The narrative has a conclusion that describes the end of an experience. | The narrative has a conclusion. | The narrative does not have a satisfactory conclusion. |

**Name(s):** _____

# My Writing Progress

How have you improved in your writing? Reread the second draft of your narrative essay. How does it compare to your final draft? When you completed your self-evaluation, you scored your second draft. Your teacher read and scored the final draft of your essay.

Review the rubric you completed for your writing along with the rubric you received from the teacher.

Write your scores in the chart below for each aspect of narrative writing.

|  | Self-Evaluation: Narrative Essay (second draft) | Teacher Evaluation: Narrative Essay (final draft) |
|---|---|---|
| Introduces Narrator and/or Character(s) |  |  |
| Introduces Situation and Setting |  |  |
| Describes Actions or Events in Order |  |  |
| Uses Dialogue and Description |  |  |
| Includes Details |  |  |
| Uses Transition Words |  |  |
| Has a Satisfactory Conclusion |  |  |

1.  Which areas show the greatest increase, or amount of improvement?

    _____

2.  Which areas show some improvement?

    _____

3.  If there are any areas with lower scores on the second narrative (final draft), why do you think this happened?

    _____

    _____

4.  How could you continue to strengthen your narrative writing?

    _____

    _____

5.  What do you notice overall about the progression of your writing over time based on the scores reflected here?

    _____

    _____

# Writing Topics

## ➤ Opinion/Argumentative Writing

### Module 1:  Public Parks
- Favorite amusement park
- Most unusual play park
- Features that should be included in kids' parks
- A type of park you'd most like to visit (e.g., scenic, amusement, water, skate, historic, theme, animal)
- A place that should be made into a national park or historic site
- Why urban parks are/are not practical in today's society
- Why botanical parks are/are not a wise investment of resources
- Why communities need parks

### Module 2:  New Transportation Technology
- Autonomous vehicles
- High-speed trains
- Hover technology
- Hyperloop train
- Magnetic transportation technology
- Car sharing
- Helicopters
- Robotics in transportation
- Alternative fuels for vehicles (electric, fuel cell [FCV], hydrogen, ethanol, biodiesel, etc.)

## ➤ Informative/Explanatory Writing

### Module 3:  Alternate Energy Sources
- Solar power
- Wind power
- Hydropower
- Geothermal power
- Tidal power
- Biogas
- Nuclear power
- The history of a particular energy source
- How a particular type of alternative energy works
- How students can use alternate energy sources

## ➤ Informative/Explanatory Writing *(cont.)*

### Module 4: Polar Change and Exploration

- Climate change
- Global warming vs. climate cycles
- South Pole/North Pole
- Polar exploration
- Earth "wobble"
- Polar vortex

---

## ➤ Narrative Writing

### Module 5: Drones

- Military drones
- Drone racing
- Drone sporting event
- Drones in the future
- A day in the life of a drone pilot
- Experience being observed by a drone (e.g., traffic safety)
- Experience observing a drone surveying something (e.g., crops, traffic)
- Using drones to make maps
- Using drones to take photographs or gather evidence
- Using drones to carry packages or messages
- Using drones to identify critical information for fighting forest fires
- Using drones for medical purposes
- Using drones for agricultural purposes
- Using drones for natural disaster management

### Module 6: Weather-Related Experiences

- Experience with unusual weather types
- Experience with weather affecting activities
- Experience with weather affecting nature
- How weather affects other areas of our lives
- Why people read or watch weather forecasts

# Meeting Standards

Each passage and activity meets one or more of the following Common Core State Standards © Copyright 2010. National Governors Association Center for Best Practices and Council of Chief State School Officers. All rights reserved. For more information about the Common Core State Standards, go to *http://www.corestandards.org/* or *http://www.teachercreated.com/standards/*.

| Reading: Literature | Activities |
|---|---|
| **Key Ideas and Details** ||
| **RL.4.1:** Refer to details and examples in a text when explaining what the text says explicitly and when drawing inferences from the text. | Understanding Opinion Writing (M1) <br> The Benefits of Botanical Gardens (M1) <br> Characteristics of a Narrative Paragraph (M5) <br> A Logical Conclusion (M5) <br> Drones for Everyone (M5) <br> View from a Drone: A Review of Narrative Writing (M5) <br> Beginnings (M6) <br> Narrative Writing: Another Look (M6) |
| **RL.4.3:** Describe in depth a character, setting, or event in a story or drama, drawing on specific details in the text (e.g., a character's thoughts, words, or actions). | A Logical Conclusion (M5) <br> Narrative Writing: Another Look (M6) |

| Reading: Informational Text | Activities |
|---|---|
| **Key Ideas and Details** ||
| **RI.4.1:** Refer to details and examples in a text when explaining what the text says explicitly and when drawing inferences from the text. | Exciting Wooden Roller Coasters (M1) <br> Vehicles Without Drivers (M2) <br> Review (M2) <br> Informative Paragraphs (M3) <br> Solar Power (M3) <br> Geothermal Energy (M3) <br> The Wonder of Hydropower (M3) <br> Polar Exploration (M4) <br> North & South (M4) <br> North Pole Changes (M4) <br> A Closer Look (M4) |
| **RI.4.2:** Determine the main idea of a text and explain how it is supported by key details; summarize the text. | Understanding Opinion Writing (M1) <br> Topic Sentences that Stand Out (M1) <br> Vehicles Without Drivers (M2) <br> Informative Paragraphs (M3) <br> Renewable Energy from Nature (M3) <br> Concluding Sentences: Read and Write (M3) <br> North Pole Changes (M4) <br> A Closer Look (M4) |
| **Craft and Structure** ||
| **RI.4.5:** Describe the overall structure (e.g., chronology, comparison, cause/effect, problem/solution) of events, ideas, concepts, or information in a text or part of a text. | Informative Paragraphs (M3) <br> Geothermal Energy (M3) <br> The Wonder of Hydropower (M3) <br> A Closer Look (M4) |
| **Integration of Knowledge and Ideas** ||
| **RI.4.8:** Explain how an author uses reasons and evidence to support particular points in a text. | Exciting Wooden Roller Coasters (M1) <br> Vehicles Without Drivers (M2) <br> Informative Paragraphs (M3) <br> Solar Power (M3) <br> North Pole Changes (M4) <br> A Closer Look (M4) |

# Meeting Standards (cont.)

| Writing | Activities |
|---|---|
| **Text Types and Purposes** | |
| **W.4.1:** Write opinion pieces on topics or texts, supporting a point of view with reasons and information. | My Opinion About Parks (M1)<br>So Many Reasons (M1)<br>Using My Senses (M1)<br>Reasons for My Opinion (M1)<br>Opinions and Concluding Sentences (M1)<br>Restating or Explaining (M1)<br>Evaluating My Writing (M1)<br>Publish a Final Draft (M1)<br>Let's Discuss Transportation (M2)<br>My Ideas About Transportation Technology (M2)<br>Moving in a Forward Direction (M2)<br>Reasons and Evidence (M2)<br>Comparing Arguments (M2)<br>The Right Conclusion (M2)<br>Practice Writing a Concluding Paragraph (M2)<br>Opposing Viewpoints (M2) |
| **W.4.2:** Write informative/explanatory texts to examine a topic and convey ideas and information clearly. | Ideas that Go Together (M3)<br>Plan Your Paragraph (M3)<br>Solar Power Words (M3)<br>Details About My Topic (M3)<br>Connecting Ideas (M3)<br>Concluding Sentences: Read and Write (M3)<br>A Different Perspective (M3)<br>Second Draft and Self-Evaluation (M3)<br>Planning My Essay (M4)<br>Structure for My Essay (M4)<br>North & South (M4)<br>My Polar Trek (M4)<br>The End Is in Sight (M4)<br>A Captivating Conclusion (M4)<br>A Reader's Perspective (M4)<br>Second Draft and Self-Evaluation (M4) |
| **W.4.3:** Write narratives to develop real or imagined experiences or events using effective technique, descriptive details, and clear event sequences. | Let Me Introduce You (M5)<br>Orient Your Reader (M5)<br>My Narrative Event Chart (M5)<br>Descriptive Details (M5)<br>Narrative Action (M5)<br>Narrative that Flows (M5)<br>The End (M5)<br>First Draft and Peer Review (M5)<br>View from a Drone: A Review of Narrative Writing (M5)<br>Building a Narrative (M6)<br>Beginnings (M6)<br>Weather Report (M6)<br>Rain or Shine (M6)<br>Steps in Your Experience (M6)<br>In Conclusion (M6)<br>Powerful Endings (M6)<br>Making Connections (M6)<br>Second Draft and Self-Evaluation (M6) |

# Meeting Standards *(cont.)*

| Writing *(cont.)* | Activities |
|---|---|
| **Production and Distribution of Writing** | |
| **W.4.4:** Produce clear and coherent writing in which the development and organization are appropriate to task, purpose, and audience. | Publish a Final Draft (M1)<br>Second Draft and Self-Evaluation (M2)<br>Hybrid Vehicles (M2)<br>Second Draft and Self-Evaluation (M3)<br>First Draft and Peer Review (M4)<br>Second Draft and Self-Evaluation (M4)<br>Second Draft and Self-Evaluation (M5)<br>Ticket to the Finals (M5)<br>First Draft and Peer Review (M6) |
| **W.4.5:** With guidance and support from peers and adults, develop and strengthen writing as needed by planning, revising, and editing. | Friendly Feedback (M1)<br>Evaluating My Writing (M1)<br>Comparing Evaluations (M1)<br>Comparing Arguments (M2)<br>Opposing Viewpoints (M2)<br>Second Draft and Self-Evaluation (M2)<br>Evaluating My Opinion Essay (M2)<br>Concluding Sentences: Read and Write (M3)<br>A Different Perspective (M3)<br>Second Draft and Self-Evaluation (M3)<br>Writing Conventions (M3)<br>Powerful Writing (M3)<br>Planning My Essay (M4)<br>The End Is in Sight (M4)<br>A Reader's Perspective (M4)<br>Changes for the Better (M4)<br>Narrative that Flows (M5)<br>The End (M5)<br>Pre-flight Checklist (M5)<br>Second Draft and Self-Evaluation (M5)<br>Ticket to the Finals (M5)<br>Graphing My Scores (M5)<br>Building a Narrative (M6)<br>In Conclusion (M6)<br>First Draft and Peer Review (M6)<br>My Writing Progress (M6) |
| **W.4.6:** With some guidance and support from adults, use technology, including the Internet, to produce and publish writing as well as to interact and collaborate with others; demonstrate sufficient command of keyboarding skills to type a minimum of one page in a single sitting. | Publish a Final Draft (M1)<br>Second Draft and Self-Evaluation (M2)<br>Final Draft (M3)<br>Ticket to the Finals (M5)<br>Second Draft and Self-Evaluation (M6) |
| **Research to Build and Present Knowledge** | |
| **W.4.7:** Conduct short research projects that build knowledge through investigation of different aspects of a topic. | Ideas that Go Together (M3)<br>Plan Your Paragraph (M3)<br>Details About My Topic (M3)<br>Planning My Essay (M4)<br>Structure for My Essay (M4)<br>Weather Report (M6) |
| **W.4.8:** Recall relevant information from experiences or gather relevant information from print and digital sources; take notes and categorize information, and provide a list of sources. | Reasons and Evidence (M2)<br>Plan Your Paragraph (M3)<br>Structure for My Essay (M4)<br>Orient Your Reader (M5)<br>Weather Report (M6) |

# Meeting Standards (cont.)

| Speaking & Listening | Activities |
|---|---|
| **Comprehension and Collaboration** | |
| **SL.4.1:** Engage effectively in a range of collaborative discussions (one-on-one, in groups, and teacher-led) with diverse partners on *grade 4 topics and texts*, building on others' ideas and expressing their own clearly. | *all* |

| Language | Activities |
|---|---|
| **Conventions of Standard English** | |
| **L.4.1:** Demonstrate command of the conventions of standard English grammar and usage when writing or speaking. | *all* |
| **L.4.2:** Demonstrate command of the conventions of standard English capitalization, punctuation, and spelling when writing. | Evaluating My Writing (M1) <br> Publish a Final Draft (M1) <br> Second Draft and Self-Evaluation (M2) <br> Writing Conventions (M3) <br> Second Draft and Self-Evaluation (M4) <br> Second Draft and Self-Evaluation (M5) <br> Ticket to the Finals (M5) <br> Second Draft and Self-Evaluation (M6) |
| **Knowledge of Language** | |
| **L.4.3:** Use knowledge of language and its conventions when writing, speaking, reading, or listening. | *all* |
| **Vocabulary Acquisition and Use** | |
| **L.4.4:** Determine or clarify the meaning of unknown and multiple-meaning words and phrases based on grade 4 reading and content, choosing flexibly from a range of strategies. | Details About My Topic (M3) <br> Descriptive Details (M5) |
| **L.4.5:** Demonstrate understanding of figurative language, word relationships, and nuances in word meanings. | Details About My Topic (M3) <br> North Pole Changes (M4) <br> Making Connections (M6) <br> Second Draft and Self-Evaluation (M6) |
| **L.4.6:** Acquire and use accurately grade-appropriate general academic and domain-specific words and phrases, including those that signal precise actions, emotions, or states of being (e.g., *quizzed, whined, stammered*) and that are basic to a particular topic (e.g., *wildlife, conservation,* and *endangered* when discussing animal preservation). | Using My Senses (M1) <br> Publish a Final Draft (M1) <br> Second Draft and Self-Evaluation (M2) <br> Solar Power Words (M3) <br> First Draft and Peer Review (M4) <br> Second Draft and Self-Evaluation (M4) <br> North Pole Changes (M4) <br> Descriptive Details (M5) <br> Ticket to the Finals (M5) <br> Making Connections (M6) <br> Second Draft and Self-Evaluation (M6) |